Dylan's Faith

T.K. Chapin

Dylan's Faith

Branch Publishing

Copyright © 2015 T.K. Chapin

All rights reserved.

ISBN-13:
978-1515083528

ISBN-10:
1515083527

DEDICATION

Dedicated to my father, his faith by example has changed my life forever.

CONTENTS

DEDICATION iv

CONTENTS vi

ACKNOWLEDGMENTS i

Prologue 1

December 01, 2010 4

December 02, 2010 18

December 24, 2010 27

December 31, 2010 42

January 14, 2011 55

January 25, 2011 67

February 10, 2011 81

February 11, 2011 95

February 14, 2011 118

February 15, 2011 125

June 01, 2011 136

June 02, 2011 149

June 03, 2011 162

June 15, 2011	178
June 19, 2011	189
June 22, 2011	201
June 26, 2011	212
November 14, 2011	216
November 14, 2066	230
Other Books	236
Author's Note	238
ABOUT THE AUTHOR	239

ACKNOWLEDGMENTS

First and foremost, I want to thank God. God's salvation through the death, burial and resurrection of Jesus Christ gives us all the ability to have a personal relationship with the creator of the Universe.

I also want to thank my wife. She's my muse and my inspiration. A wonderful wife, an amazing mother and the best person I have ever met. She's great and has always stood by me with every decision I have made along life's way.

I'd like to thank my editors and early readers for helping me along the way. I also want to thank all of my friends and extended family for the support. It's a true blessing to have every person I know in my life.

.

PROLOGUE

Life has a funny way of taking us down roads we never thought we'd travel. Sometimes we might be on a long stretch of road that never seems to end. Other times we can't keep up with life's turns, hills and construction zones. No matter what part of the journey we're on, each road can lead to the unexpected. A little detour here, a wrong turn there, it's all just part of the experience. When the love of my life showed up, there was no big billboard alongside the road letting me know it was the one. Thankfully, God was in my passenger seat when she came into my life, and if it wasn't for Him, I might have passed her by. My faith has been a large part of my life, and God has helped through more struggles than I can count.

This brittle and fragile body of mine is wearing out with every passing day, but I take comfort as I sit in the same rocking chair that my beloved rocked our children to sleep in. I take not only comfort in the chair, but the overwhelming peace that the Lord has given me. This chair I had crafted with my own two hands years ago and over the years it's worn out much like my body. But my faith never ages, never ceases, and never grows weary. And while my body seems to have new aches and pains in areas I never knew existed, my God never weakens. He's the same as He was yesterday as He is today and that He will be tomorrow.

Glancing at the picture of my late wife between my cracking fingers, I smile and laugh a little to myself as I let my thumb cross over it. What I used to fear, death, I now look forward to. The day I pass onto glory will be the day when I finally get some rest for these old bones and see loved ones who have passed on. And best of all, I'll meet Jesus. What a glorious and wonderful day that will be. I have no regrets for the life I have lived. I wasn't perfect by any means, but I have lived a satisfying and full life. I have loved another with all my heart and have raised my family in the house of the Lord.

My successes in life, both in business and in family, I contribute fully to my Savior Jesus Christ. It's been through His grace, comfort and love that I've been able to live this blessed life. It hasn't all been butterflies and roses by any means, but regardless, I have loved every moment of it. If it weren't for God being by my side in times of struggle, my life would have turned out much differently, I'm sure of it.

All my children have long left the home and have gone on to start their own families. I do hear from each one of them from time to time and see them on holidays, but I often reminisce of the days of their youth. Those years might be in the past, but the memories are what comforts me in my old age.

Who am I? I'm Dylan Holden. You won't find my face on the front page of a magazine and you won't see my struggles on an episode of some reality television show. No, my story lives in the recesses of my memory. I'm an ordinary man who was able to rely on my faith in God to endure what felt like the impossible.

As I sit here in the tranquility of my solitude, I reflect back on the days of when I first met the love of my life. That whole period of time I relied heavily on my faith. Without it, I would have never been able to live the life that I have now. Those days were so long ago, but when I close my eyes for long enough, I can transport back in time and it's as if I were there in that transformational part of my life. I can feel my youth return to my bones and my strength to my body. I can even see my old house I shared with my brother Chris out in Chattaroy and my old shop around back. Oh yes, it all seems just like it happened yesterday. The winter of two thousand ten was when it all began.

DECEMBER 01, 2010

It was one of the coldest winters in forty years for Chattaroy, Washington, but the space heater out in my shop kept the frostbite from setting in while I toiled away on the table I was crafting for Mr. Nortaggen, better known as Floyd around town. He was one of the farmers out here who I became good acquaintances with over the years. His son Levi and I knew each other through our youth, but became better friends after graduating High School.

This particular table I was working on was not just one of the typical pieces of furniture I crafted to sell down at the local feed store; this one was a favor. Levi provided me with an old photograph that came from Floyd's childhood, and in that photograph was a long and elegant triple-pedestal dining room table that had been in the family for over fifty years. I always admired its beauty the times I had been over there. A fire at Floyd's house last year burned up the family heirloom, and just a few months ago is when Levi approached me about making a new table for the family. He said he wanted the table to be an anniversary gift to Floyd and Margret for thirty years of marriage. I gladly accepted the request, and I viewed it as a good challenge for myself.

As I applied the primer to the table top that measured just a smidge over six feet, I was interrupted by my brother Chris. He came barreling through the shop door panting heavily. Chris was a couple years younger than me; just twenty three at the time, but his strength about matched my own.

"Roy just called; he said they had another pack of coyotes come down from the hill last night and kill another sheep."

"You heading over there?" I asked.

"Yeah, did you want to go?"

Looking down at my table, I replied, "Let me finish up this coat of primer and then we'll head over."

"Okay, I'll go load the guns into the truck."

"Sounds like a plan, Brother."

Chris took off back through the shop door, shutting the door behind him. Turning my attention back to work, I continued my strokes of primer carefully, being sure not to leave any streaks behind.

We were able to find the coyotes and take care of the problem. After we put our guns back in my truck's cab, we ventured up the sidewalk to Roy's farmhouse to tell him the issue had been resolved.

Kicking our boots off on the porch and hanging up our coats, we came into the kitchen through the side door. Roy was sitting at the table, with his hands folded. Roy was a role model I looked up to for my own life. Strong in his faith with the Lord, he never wavered in his beliefs and stayed rooted in God.

"You get them coyotes?" Roy asked, as we joined him at the kitchen table. Glancing out the window, I nodded. "We sure did. We had to high tail it up around the corner of the hill to catch the pack, but we got them all."

"Those coyotes had no chance with Dylan's sharp eye and quick trigger finger," Chris said, patting me on the back.

Grinning, I shook my head. "You got a couple of them also, Chris; you can't let me take all the credit."

"Regardless... you guys did a great job," Roy said. "Thank you."

Jess came into the kitchen and fetched a glass from the cupboard. She was my friend Levi's wife and Roy's granddaughter. She was pregnant and due in just a few months. After pouring herself a glass of orange juice from the pitcher in the fridge, she took a seat at the table. "How are you guys?" She asked. "We haven't seen you two around very often this winter."

"I've been working on that table," I replied.

"Oh yeah, Levi is excited about that. How's it coming along?"

"Pretty good, just working on the priming and staining now," I replied. "Speaking of Levi, why's he not back from Colville yet?"

Jess shook her head. "He got snowed in up there. The roads are bad, and what sucks is he didn't even buy any cattle on this trip."

"That's a tremendous waste of time," Chris said.

"Exactly," Jess replied with a sigh.

"He should have gone to Quincy. They had an auction going on also--way better selection up there," Roy said.

"Oh well," she replied taking a sip of her juice. Jumping a little in her seat, she smiled, "One of them kicked!"

"Them?" I asked.

She covered her mouth. "Oops… we were keeping it a secret, but that's out now! We're having twins!"

"Grats, bet Levi's looking forward to that," I replied.

"Congratulations!" Chris said.

"Thank you, we are excited. Few more months and

they'll be here!" Jess said, beaming with a smile.

Glancing up at the clock, Chris cleared his throat. "We better get going, Dylan. I'm getting hungry."

Peering up at the clock above the sink, I nodded and rose to my feet. "Crazy how looking at the time can make you hungry, Brother," I replied smiling. Looking over at Roy, I shook his hand and said, "Let us know if you have any more coyote problems and Levi isn't around."

"Of course. Why don't you stay and have a meal with us? It's the least I can do," Roy replied.

Shaking my head, I said, "Thanks for the offer, but Chris here has been itching to see his little lady friend."

"Alright. That's fine, just thought I'd offer," Roy replied with a grin. "Take care of yourselves."

Arriving at the Wagon Wheel, we were greeted by Elly, Chris's girlfriend. She was one of the servers there and had been ever since she graduated from high school and quit her job at the convenience store.

"Heya, gorgeous," Chris said, laying a kiss on Elly's lips.

Squirming, she laughed as she replied, "I'm working. You can't do that." She pushed him back gently.

"Alright, it's just hard to keep my hands off you," he replied smiling.

"Bar or dining area?" she asked grabbing menus from the side of the podium.

"Bar's fine," Chris replied.

"Let's do the dining area, Bro. It's always loud in the bar with the TV's and whatnot, I just want to relax."

"Alright, fine," he replied.

We followed Elly over into the dining area and she led us to a booth. Setting our menus down on the table as we took a seat, she asked, "Pitcher?"

"Yep," Chris replied.

"I'll let your server know. Should be the new girl Trisha. Be nice." Elly took off back towards the front entrance. Chris's eyes watched as she walked away.

"How's that possible promotion at work going?" I asked as I looked at my menu. Chris was up for a promotion at the Chattaroy Feed Store; it was between himself and another worker named Tyler. They had both been working at the store for almost two years and the assistant manager had plans to move to another state. Ever since he put his one-month notice in just a week ago, it'd been a fight between Tyler and Chris for the job.

"It's going... it's so early, we have no idea who's going to get it."

"Who's better buds with Ken?" I asked.

"Well Ken hangs out with Tyler a lot more outside of

work, but I work a whole heck of a lot harder than he."

"Sounds like Tyler has the upper hand on this one."

"C'mon, Dylan. My hard work has to count for something!"

"Maybe, but if I had to bet money, I'd say it is whoever is better buds with the manager; it's all about who you know."

"We'll see," he replied.

Looking at the menu, I mulled over in my mind what I wanted to eat. I had eaten there more times than I could count, but still needed to look at the menu to figure out what my meal would be. Then I spotted what sounded delicious, a home-style breakfast. Bacon, eggs, hash browns and a couple pieces of toast on the side. "I'm going with the House specialty breakfast," I said, closing my menu.

Chris set his menu down on the edge of the table.

"What about you?" I asked.

"Steak and potato." Chris always ordered the same thing for dinner when we went there; not sure why he ever looked at the menu.

Suddenly our server came over with the pitcher of beer and two ice cold glasses. She had beautiful flowing brown hair and piercing emerald green eyes. And then when she spoke, she revealed a gorgeous smile to complete the package. "How you boy's doing tonight? My name is Trisha and I'll be your server tonight."

"We're good… so you're new in town?" I replied.

"Yes I am." She pulled out her order pad. "What can I get ya'll to eat? Or did you need a little more time?"

It took everything in me not to stare at her. She was pretty. "I'll take a chicken salad," I said.

Chris looked at me funny, tilting his head. "You didn't say you wanted that earlier…"

"I changed my mind," I replied. "Just go ahead and order, Chris…"

Shaking his head, he said, "Alrighty, I'll take the steak and potato."

"And how did you want that steak?"

"Medium-rare, oh and load up the potato please, everything on it," he replied.

"Okay. And did you guys want anything to drink other than the beer? We have soda, ice tea, lemonade."

I replied, "I'll take a water. Here, I don't need a glass," I said, handing her the beer glass back.

"Alright, I'll go ahead and get that order in for you two." She grabbed the extra glass, menus, and left our table.

Leaning across the table, Chris asked, "Dude, why'd you get a salad? Trying to impress the newbie?" He laughed.

Shaking my head, I said, "I just changed my mind." I looked up and spotted Trisha across the restaurant, taking another table's order. I couldn't help but keep looking over at her. She was drop-dead gorgeous. Chris looked over his shoulder to see what was keeping my attention.

He turned back to me and smiled, "She's hot, huh?"

"She's okay." Wanting to change the subject, I asked, "What's the temperature getting down to tonight?"

"I don't know... Why don't you ask for her number, dude?" He leaned in closer. "I bet you can't do it."

Shaking my head, I replied, "You're right, I can't." I laughed. "I don't want to hit on our server. That doesn't seem right." Chris grabbed the pitcher and poured himself a tall glass of cold beer. Bringing the glass to his lips, he proceeded to chug the entire thing.

"Wow!" He replied with a loud clap. "This night's going to be good! I can feel it in my bones!"

"Take it easy," I said, watching him pour another glass.

"I know... just getting relaxed. Chill." Chris had a drinking problem if you asked anyone around town--well that's with the exception of himself; he'd never admit it. Quite a few nights resulted in us both fist-fighting with other guys at the Wagon Wheel. A few times even resulted in the cops showing up.

Leaning across the table, I said, "Do you really want to end up in another fight?"

"Why not?" Chris asked with his eyebrows raised. "It's the only time I get a chance to see our father."

Shaking my head, I replied, "You just might be as sick as him, you know that?"

"Oh please..." Chris said as he took a sip of his beer.

"Save me the psychoanalysis. I was kidding. I fight because it's in my nature to right the wrong in the world."

A group of burly looking guys who I hadn't ever seen before sat at a table across the restaurant. Chris kept his eyes locked on them as they kept looking over at us. He downed three more glasses of beer before the food finally arrived.

As Trisha set my salad down in front of me, I felt a feeling of stupidity come over me. I really didn't even want the salad. I had just ordered it to show her I'm healthy. Trying to impress a girl by what I'm eating? That was silly I thought to myself. "Thank you," I said, smiling at her. She grinned at me as she placed the steak in front of Chris.

"This looks delicious, thank you," Chris replied, picking up his silverware.

"Enjoy," she said, walking away from the table.

Looking up at Chris, I saw his eyes begin to get that red glaze over them that they do when he's getting buzzed on his way to being drunk. I reached for my water and took a drink. "You better slow down…"

"I'll be okay dude, don't worry about me. This food will help soak it up, chill out."

As we ate our dinners we could hear the group of guys snickering from a distance. Judging by Chris's cringing he must have been able to catch part of their conversation. "Are they talking about us?" I asked, leaning across the table.

"They're saying we're a couple of hicks from the back country."

"Really?" I asked, surprised. I tried to listen in on the table and I couldn't hear anything over the music in the restaurant. "I'll be right back." Getting up from the booth, I headed towards the bathroom and stopped in the hallway to listen in on the table.

"How's the soup?" a guy at the table asked.

"Fine," another guy replied.

"My steak is a little overdone, but it's okay," another guy added.

Shaking my head I walked back to my table. Taking a seat back down with Chris, I said, "Its fine... they are just talking about their food."

Chris glared their direction as he replied, "I don't think so. Who laughs about their food?"

"Maybe someone said something funny? Just eat your food and ignore them." I picked up my fork and began eating my salad. Chris laughed at me a little when he saw my less-than-satisfied expression as I ate my leafy green dinner.

As we were leaving the restaurant, the guys from the table were out in the parking lot getting into their car. "What do you hicks do for fun?" The tall and muscular guy asked from over at his car.

"Excuse me?" I said, stopping before I got into the truck.

"I said what do you hicks do for fun out here?" He asked smirking as he came over to the truck.

Chris shut his door and joined my side with his arms

crossed. He was drunk by now. Leaning over into my ear, he said, "Told you they called us hicks…"

"You understand calling us hicks is offensive, right?" I asked hoping the man didn't mean to offend us.

The man spat on the ground and laughed a little. "Hillbilly… whatever you inbreeds like to be called, I don't really care." He pushed my shoulder.

"Don't touch me," I replied firmly.

Chris stepped in between us and got up on his toes and into the man's face. "You should leave."

The man laughed, looking down at Chris. "Or what?" The other couple of guys from his car came up behind him. He pushed Chris backwards, causing his step to stagger into me.

Oh great, I thought to myself as Chris regained his balance. Cocking his arm back, Chris slugged the guy right in the gut and the fight started. One of the guys from the group charged me and I side stepped and clothes-lined him to the pavement. Another guy punched me in the face and I threw my elbow into another's nose, causing it to instantly start bleeding and him to back off. Chris got slammed to the ground by the big guy and I came over and pushed the big guy off Chris, causing him to stagger.

As I helped Chris up, he said, "Behind you!"

Turning, I grabbed the guy I first laid out on the pavement and threw him by me right into the front of my truck. The bigger guy decked me in the face causing my nose to start bleeding. Shaking my head, I cocked my arm back and slugged him in the face and Chris slugged him in the stomach.

Suddenly Missy, the bar owner, came out cocking her shot gun and firing up into the sky, stopping us all in our tracks.

"You best stop fighting in front of my restaurant or I'll call the cops."

Holding up our hands, Chris and I backed away towards our truck while the other guys scrambled to get up and head over to their car. Keeping the gun pointed at the out-of-towners, Missy waited for both our vehicles to leave.

Backing up out of the parking space, I said, "She's going to tell Dad... We're toast."

Missy was the owner of the Wagon Wheel and good friends with our father, Frank. They had a bit of a history and she was holding out on her true love, our father, coming back to her one day. She'd report all our shenanigans to him, always thinking she'd earn her way back into his good graces. But the only thing it ever accomplished, her telling our father about our fights, was a guarantee he'd be by to visit us the following day.

"Why do we let him beat us up? We can so take him on..." Chris said on the drive back home.

After wiping my nose of the blood with a napkin from the glove box, I replied, "And do what? Beat him up so he can go get a gun and just shoot us? Sounds like an awesome plan, Brother. He's just trying to correct us like he did when we were kids."

"Could he really shoot us?" Chris asked.

"He shot you in the shoulder, or did you forget that?"

Chris got quiet. "It's just stupid we can't go to the Wagon Wheel without her telling on us… Just need to go into Spokane if we want to go eat and have a beer I guess."

"Yeah, let's drive clear to Spokane just to have a drink with our meal. How about we just don't fight? Or you don't drink." Looking in the mirror I saw the blood running out of my nose and I felt another wave of stupidity rush over me. I could have stopped that fight from happening if we just got in the truck and left.

DECEMBER 02, 2010

The next day our father Frank came out to the house. Hearing the knock on the door froze us both in our footsteps. There was no way we were not going to get a little roughed up after last night's fight. Shaking my head, I checked out the window to make sure Dad didn't have a gun in his hand. He didn't.

Opening the door, I was surprised my father didn't look angry. "What's going on, Dad?"

"Aren't you going to invite me in, boy?" He asked.

Pushing open the screen door, I lowered my head as he stepped in. My heart was racing, as I feared what was to come of his visit. He looked around and then took a seat on the couch. "Look, we didn't start that fight last night-" I began to explain, but he lifted a hand to stop me from talking.

"I don't care about the fight," he said with a serious tone. "I'm done trying to whip you boys into shape. I have some news for you. Take a seat." He looked over at Chris, who was standing in the doorway that led into the kitchen. "Come sit down, Son."

"What's going on?" Chris asked, still trying to keep a length of distance between himself and Frank as he sat down in the recliner.

"I wanted to talk to you about the Silverback."

The Silverback was the inn on the outskirts of Chattaroy that sat nestled up against a beautiful and private lake. Our father Frank ran and operated it for the last twenty years. It was his pride and joy. He lived there, worked there and was all-consumed by the day-to-day operations. It had been that way ever since Mom died when we were just boys.

"What about it?" I asked.

"Your uncle Lenny's going to be taking over it soon," he replied, his eyes were glued to the floor. His voice seemed shaky and upset. This was a side of our father we never saw, and his statement made me worry.

"What, why?" Chris asked, leaning in from his seat on the recliner.

Looking up at us, he said, "I'm dying... I won't be here for more than a few more months and I need someone to take over." Dying? What? No. There wasn't any possible way my father could be dying. He looked like he always did.

"What?" I asked.

"I said, I'm dying…"

"What's wrong with you?" I asked softly.

"Degenerative heart failure…" he said before sighing heavily.

"And you'll die in three months?" I asked.

"There isn't an exact number son. I know it's troubling."

"Dad…" I said softly. "Aren't you scared? You don't even look worried."

"I'm not going to sit here and talk about emotions son."

"Of course you aren't," Chris replied curtly.

"So anyways, your uncle Lenny will be taking over it."

My sadness over the fact my only parent was going to be gone soon was eclipsed by my anger that he would not be leaving Chris and I the inn. He was betraying us. Shaking my head, I replied, "That sucks you're dying Dad… but you're going with your brother over your own two sons."

He narrowed his eyes at me. "Look at your face, Dylan." He laughed sarcastically. "It's busted up. You think you two idiots can handle running a business? You can't go more than a few weeks without getting into a fight, let alone be responsible for something for once in your life."

"That's not true. Look at this house. We bought this," I retorted.

"Yeah, with your grandmother's inheritance money. Grats, you bought something."

"At least we didn't just blow the money. You know what Dad? I'm sick of your ill-treatment towards us. You don't even come around here unless it's to teach us some twisted lesson. You don't know us or our life," I replied.

"I'd beat the snot out of you for talking that way to me if I hadn't had some real changes in my life recently… That's beside the point, I know enough to know not to give either of you two real responsibility."

Chris remained quiet as he relaxed back into the recliner. He seemed more relieved with the fact he wasn't getting roughed up by dad than he was upset about the inn or our dad dying.

"This not fair! We're your own flesh and blood!"

"Don't you raise your tone with me Dylan," he said with a clenched jaw. "You know just as well as I do that Lenny's a better fit."

Shaking my head, I could feel my blood boil inside. "That isn't right, Dad, and you know it."

"It is what it is, Son, just drop it, please. I'm trying hard to control my anger with you boys right now. Let's change the subject. What else is going on?" he asked.

After saying a quick and silent prayer for strength in the moment and for my dad, I took a deep breath and let the Lord take away my frustrations. "I'm working on a three-pedestal dining room table."

"Three-pedestal?" He asked with an eyebrow raised. "I'd be curious to see it."

"It's in the shop, I'll show you." I headed for the door and he followed close behind. Even though I loathed him at the moment, it didn't remove my desire to make him proud.

On the way back to the shop, he asked, "What made you decide to make a table this big?"

Looking back over my shoulder, I said, "Levi asked me to do it for Floyd."

"Ahh… that makes sense. That fire obliterated that table of theirs."

"Yep."

Opening the shop door, we came in and I flipped the light on. Coming over to the table top, he slid the palm of his hand across the top. I waited anxiously for his comments as he inspected the groves and details of the table. He had done woodworking for a side hobby for as long as I could remember. He had crafted much of the furniture that now furnishes the rooms at the inn. He had an amazing talent when it came to wood crafting. "Come here," he said sternly over at me.

I walked over and looked to where he was pointing. "What is it?" I asked.

"See that right there?" He asked.

"Yeah?"

He walked over to the other end of the table and motioned for me to join him. Then he pointed to another groove, "It doesn't match that depth, this is shoddy work."

I was disheartened by his comment as I rubbed my index finger against the groove. "How is it outside of that?"

"It'll do," he replied. "It's flawed, but most people won't catch it."

Nodding, my eyes stayed fixed on the groove. He noticed my disappointment in myself over the fact and patted my shoulder on the way back towards the shop door.

"Just keep practicing son and you'll get there." Another sting by the lips of my father. Why couldn't he just be proud of me? He said himself that not many people would notice it.

He and I headed out of the shop and back towards the front of the house, but he stopped along the side of the house.

"Hey Dylan, before we get back inside, I want to tell you something. But keep it between us, can you do that?" He asked.

"Sure Dad."

"I want you guys to have the inn… But your brother's fighting is out of control. I know I've been hard on you two, but that was to help you push through anything that this life throws your way. That, and I felt the need to correct your behavior."

"I can handle it, Dad. I can run the inn with ease."

"I don't think you can. You just can't seem to give your brother a good letting alone, and running off to protect your brother is going to land you in big trouble one of these days."

"What if I do leave Chris alone? Can I have it then? I can show you before… you know…"

Nodding, he replied, "I'd consider giving it to you. I want that inn to stay within our family more than anything, and you or both of you would be my first pick if I could trust you. But when I think about you running the inn right now I see you blowing it off and running down to the bar to pull your brother out of a fight… and then you are in jail and not at work… and it's just not good. Do you understand that?"

"Yes, Dad."

Smiling, he nodded. "Good. Let's head back in. I need to tell you both some more about Lenny and his arrival at the inn."

Climbing the steps of the porch, we headed back in to join Chris in the living room. "Looks good, doesn't it?" Chris asked as we took our seats back down.

Frank nodded. "Lenny's bringing an investment with him to the inn."

"What kind of investment?" I asked.

"You know the inn has been in pretty rough shape and

has needed a facelift for quite some time now," Frank said. "The changes could help get more people to visit, which was all I ever wanted."

"Why would we care, Dad? We're not getting the inn," Chris snapped back at him.

"Cool it Chris," I said. "It's still our family's inn. Even if Lenny is running it we're still going to be getting dividends on the shares we do have."

"Yep, and those shares will be worth more if we can get some good changes at the inn," Frank added.

"It's not in that bad of shape that I recall," Chris replied.

Frank shook his head, "You haven't been out there in a while. It is in pretty bad shape. We have loose floor boards, dirtiness here and there… and a lot of things are outdated and falling apart. It just needs some help getting back up to its full potential. He's going to be investing in the Silverback's future and leading that project soon."

I nodded. "That sounds… interesting. I'm a little worried what that might all entail. Do you think he can keep the feel of the inn in tact?"

"I trust him," Frank replied. "He's my brother and we've had a long talk." Looking at his watch, Frank said, "I better get going, I have an appointment in town with the doctor."

"Okay," I replied delicately. I knew my father had no desire to talk about the heart failure or the fact he was going to be leaving earth soon. He was a very private man and he'd rather talk about the plan moving forward instead of the fact he wasn't going to be around much longer. He was a planner at heart.

Chris got up and headed upstairs without saying anything more to Dad. I patted my father on the shoulder and walked with him out to his truck.

"Hey Dad," I said. My voice was a little shaky, but I cleared my throat.

Stopping, he looked at me, "Yes."

"Take care of yourself. And let Lenny know I want to help out with the renovations any way I can. It would be an honor."

He nodded. "I'll let him know."

As he climbed into the cab of his truck, I thought to myself, why's he have to keep such a strong composure? He's dying and yet didn't shed a single tear or share a single personal feeling about it with us. He had to be scared and worried about passing. I knew he wasn't a born-again believer and I worried. As he backed out, I prayed the same prayer I did every day for him. That the Lord would break into his world and reveal the awesome power, love and comfort that only God can bring. While my prayer remained the same, I couldn't help but feel it was more imperative now than ever before.

DECEMBER 24, 2010

The table for Floyd was ready. The finish I put on the table was a dark cherry red and I personally felt the table looked amazing. Levi was on his way over from Roy's with the trailer as I pushed open the bay doors of my shop. The night sky had already settled in for the evening and the shop's floodlight illuminated the snowflakes that were falling that Christmas Eve. Plumes of breath escaped my lips as I anticipated Levi's arrival.

Chris came around from the front of the house, bundled up in his checkered red and black jacket and a beanie cap. His hands were hidden away in his pockets and his steps were light as he approached the shop.

"She's finally done, eh?" He asked, coming in from the snow into the bay.

"She sure is," I smiled turning to join Chris' gaze at the table and chairs. "This is by far the most amazing thing I've ever made out here in this shop."

"It better be for the amount of time you poured into it," Chris said. Sliding his fingers across the top of the table as he walked around it, he shook his head. "This is so cool dude. You did a great job."

"Thanks. I just hope Floyd likes it. It's a little different than the photo I got... but I don't think it's a bad different."

"Where's that photo at?" Chris asked.

"Over on the wall above the workbench right over there," I said pointing.

Chris went over and looked at the photo and then back at the table. "I'd say it's an improvement." Coming back over to the table, he nodded. "Maybe you can make and sell some of these down at the feed store?"

Shaking my head, I said, "The money Levi paid for the oak isn't an investment I'd want to sit on for very long. And a table like this might take a while to sell."

"I didn't even think about waiting to sell it; you're probably right," Chris said.

"Let's get it covered up before Levi shows," I said going over to the wall to grab the blankets and tarp. Levi hadn't seen the table for the last month of work. He saw some of the shaping on the table and the chairs, but not much. He wanted to be surprised with Floyd and Margret when they see it. As Chris and I finished covering the table, Levi pulled into the driveway.

Reversing in, he backed the trailer up to the bay's opening. I came out of the shop and helped him navigate back the rest of the way in.

"I'm so excited!" Levi said, jumping out of the cab of his truck and hurrying back to us.

Nodding, I smiled. "Hope you all like how it turned out."

"I have every bit of confidence in you," Levi said patting my shoulder.

We all helped load the table onto the trailer and strapped it in with tie downs. Chris and I even wrapped the chairs up tight, mostly to keep them from getting damaged from the snow, but it also had to do with it all being a big surprise.

After loading, Chris and I jumped into my truck and followed Levi over to Floyd's for the big reveal at the Christmas Eve celebration. Floyd and Roy's family do a gift exchange on Christmas Eve and back a few years ago they started including us. It was nice to be included since we didn't have much of our own family around for the holidays.

Arriving to Floyd's house, Levi was able to pull the trailer around the milk house undetected. I just parked my truck in the driveway in front of the house. Levi came running from the milk house to catch up to us before we went inside.

"How'd you manage to not have the dogs barking and Margret and Floyd out here greeting us? They seem to always do that," I said.

"Jeremy and Craig are in on the surprise, so I made sure to let them know to keep the dogs locked up in the milk house and Floyd and Margret down in the basement with music pretty loud."

Chris and I both laughed. Chris said, "That's genius, you went through a lot of work to keep it a surprise as long as possible."

"I can't take the credit, Jess came up with the plan," He replied grinning as we headed inside.

"Speaking of, is she coming?" I asked.

"Yeah, she had to go pick up her cousin from the airport. She's coming to stay with us for a while on the farm. I tried talking Jess into letting me go instead, being pregnant and all, but she insisted on going."

"Ahh… I see," I replied.

Walking inside the house, Craig was coming up the stairs and he looked relieved to see us. Whispering at us, he said, "Thank heavens you are here, they've been getting cranky down there!" Craig is thirty two and lives in Spokane with his wife Melanie. He has a son and two girls. He works at the biggest plastic factory in the area, Spokane Plastics, as a traveling sales representative.

"Thanks for keeping them away," Levi said grinning. "It's going to be awesome."

"You still haven't seen it?" Craig asked.

"Nope," Levi said.

Craig turned to us. "Is it pretty nice? Levi showed me some of the work you've done in the past... pretty impressive, Dylan."

"Thanks," I replied. "I think it turned out nicely. I'm glad I was fortunate enough to make a career out of my passion."

Coming up the stairs, Jeremy, Floyd and Margret all smiled at us.

Jeremy was thirty three and lived with his wife and two daughters in Spokane. He also works out at the plastic factory with Craig, but he's one of the shift leaders on the factory floor.

"Oh, jeez!" Margret said smacking Jeremy's arm. "Look at what you two boys did! I don't even have the punch ready and we have guests!" Almost running, Margret continued past us and towards the kitchen. "I'm so sorry Dylan and Chris; the boys were keeping us downstairs listening to silly Christmas music really loud..."

I laughed. "That's okay, we just barely got here."

"I know. I just hate to not be prepared for guests!" She said, as she pulled out the fruit punch and lemon-lime soda from the fridge in the kitchen.

"Where are the women who put up with you two? And the kids?" I asked looking at Craig and Jeremy.

Craig laughed a little and replied, "The kids are downstairs playing and the women are on their way here. They decided to grab a few last-minute Christmas gifts."

I nodded. "Last-minute shopping on Christmas Eve is always fun."

"Punch is ready and I'm setting out some finger foods here in a minute for you all to enjoy while the ham finishes in the oven. The girls should be here soon and then we can open gifts," Margret said from the kitchen.

The women soon arrived and conversation filled the air around the living room as the fire crackled in the fireplace. We were just waiting on Jess and her cousin to arrive. I, myself, was deep in a conversation with Craig about his latest visit to Odessa, Texas for business when suddenly it was interrupted by a knock on the door.

All the adults went silent for a moment as they looked over to see Jess come through. That baby bump of hers was growing and I greeted her with a smile across the room before I directed my attention back to my conversation with Craig. Then a woman came in behind Jess, capturing my attention once more. I suddenly was a loss for words in the middle of my conversation with Craig. I couldn't help but lust after the woman's beauty. It had an intoxicating effect on me. My pulse quickened, my palms went sweaty and I felt an intense and burning desire for her inside of me. She was more beautiful than any woman I had ever seen. Curly, flowing blonde hair dangled perfectly next to her cheeks, and her eyes were an inviting ocean blue. She smiled, revealing perfect white teeth. I couldn't keep my eyes off her as she spoke with Jess.

"Dylan?" Craig said breaking into my thoughts.

Trying to shake off my desire, I turned back to Craig. "Sorry about that…"

"You were saying?" Craig asked leaning in to listen a little better since the room was growing louder with conversation.

"Umm… yeah… I'm lost." I laughed, shaking my head.

"Dylan, come meet Jess's cousin," Levi said over near the door.

Craig looked over at them and then nodded to me. "Go ahead, man. Our conversation can wait."

Standing up, I walked over to Levi. I felt nervous as I got closer to the one that ignited this fire inside of me. Part lust and part curiosity kept me on the path towards her. She was lingering near Levi, right between him and Jess. As I made my way across the living room, I said a prayer to myself for God to help me. I felt lust for this beautiful woman and I needed God's strength. Accidently tripping over Kelsey, the three year old who was playing on the carpet below my feet, I said, "Oops!" as I hopped out of the way, nearly stepping on one of her fingers.

Finally arriving over at Levi, Jess and this woman, I extended a hand to greet her. "Hi, I'm Dylan. How do you do?" How do you do? What was I thinking? That line was terrible. I could feel my cheeks go red with embarrassment.

"I'm glad to be off that airplane," she replied smiling. "I'm Allison." Placing a hand on the little boy and girl who accompanied her, she continued, "This is Sammy and Olivia, my children." I was so intoxicated with her beauty; I had failed to notice the children earlier.

"Nice to meet you all." I smiled down at the children and then back up at her. "You're happy to be off the plane? I take it you're not much for flying?"

"No, never have been…" Bumping her shoulder into Jess's, she continued, "Probably why I don't get out to Chattaroy often."

"Yeah, didn't even make the wedding, brat." Jess laughed.

"I don't care for flying either… Where'd you fly in from?" I asked.

"We're from Atlanta," she replied.

Jess bent down to Sammy and Olivia. "I need to take your mom into the kitchen for a moment. Could you stay here?"

Both children remained respectfully quiet, but nodded to Jess. They seemed like well behaved children compared to some of the kids I had seen in public.

"How old are you, Olivia?" I asked as I bent my knee to meet them both at eye level.

"I'm six. And Sammy's five, but he's shy. Where'd our mom go?" she replied. Sammy shuffled his steps and hid behind Olivia.

"She just had to go into the kitchen in the next room over. That's neat—you're six years old." Leaning to one side to see Sammy a little better, I asked, "Did you ride on a big airplane?"

He hid his face behind his sister more.

She looked at me, "See, told you, shy."

I smiled at her. "I guess you're right." Standing up, I began to turn and leave. "Guess he wouldn't be interested in a magic trick either," I said over my shoulder as I glanced back at Sammy and saw his little brown eyes peek out from behind his sister.

"What trick?" he asked curiously.

Turning back to the two of them, I bent back down. I retrieved the wooden coin I kept in my pocket and held it up to him to see. "This coin is magic."

"How?" he asked, stepping out from behind Olivia.

Holding it in my palm, I said, "Now you see the coin…" Closing my palm, I let it slide down my sleeve without him seeing and said, "Now you don't." Opening my hand, it was gone.

His eyes widened. "Where'd it go?"

"Where all the magic coins go," I smiled, standing up.

"No, really, where'd it go?" Olivia asked.

"Don't you know that a magician never reveals his tricks?" I asked.

"Why not?" Olivia asked.

"Because the magic would be lost."

"Olivia, Sammy, you can come in here now," Allison called out from the kitchen to them.

"I'll see you two around," I said and went to go sit back down with Craig.

"You're really good with kids," Craig said. Leaning in closer to me, he continued, "There's just something special about having your DNA running around your house. You really ought to put yourself out there, Dylan, and find a lady to settle down with."

"I would love to meet someone, but I'm waiting on the Lord to bring the right woman into my life. I'm hoping all I have to do is see the woman and God will whisper in my ear, she's the one."

Craig laughed. "If God starts verbally speaking to you, let me know and I'll check you into a mental institution."

I laughed. "You know what I mean."

"Yeah, I do, but don't let yourself get in your own way, Dylan."

I nodded. "I won't."

"Time to exchange gifts!" Margret said coming into the living room. Resting her hand on Floyd's shoulder as he sat in his green recliner, she continued, "Parents find a seat, children, find your parents and sit near their feet."

The women came and joined their husbands on the couches and in folding chairs, while Allison looked a bit lost. "Here's a spot," Craig said as he slid down to let her sit on the couch between us. Shaking my head, I laughed a little, knowing what he was attempting to do.

Taking a seat, she asked, "What's so funny?"

"Nothing," I said.

"Okay," Margret said. "Now Molly is the second oldest grandchild and since it's her turn to hand out gifts, she can take a seat right by the tree." Molly beamed with a smile as she stood up from Jeremy's feet and sat next to all the presents. "Go ahead and grab one, then hand it to that person. And FYI there are gifts for everyone, blood or not. We are all family one way or another! Enjoy!" Margret smiled as she sat on the arm rest of the chair that Floyd was sitting in.

By the end of the exchange, the floor wasn't visible in any area of the living room, thanks to all the wrapping paper strewn throughout. Kids were playing with their new toys and adults were hugging and thanking each other for their thoughtful gifts. My gift, which was from Floyd, was in a small box and still wrapped sitting on the bookshelf behind me. In all the excitement of the exchange, I had put it aside to watch as all the thankfulness poured out from the family.

"Aren't you going to open your gift?" Allison asked.

"Yeah," I replied. Reaching behind me, I smiled at Allison as I reached up and grabbed the box. Turning back to face everyone, I noticed Chris with a grin on his face across the room. "What are you smiling about Chris?" I laughed.

He shook his head.

Undoing the wrapping paper carefully, I slid out the box and popped off the top. Inside, lying in the cotton at the bottom was a keychain. It read: Got wood? Allison was looking in the box also and got a strange look on her face.

"What is that about?" she asked, looking up at me. When our eyes met, I felt a jolt rush through me.

Floyd, Chris and Levi began busting up laughing as I pulled the keychain out. Margret looked confused as she asked, "What's it say?"

Flashing Margret the keychain, she said, "That's highly inappropriate!" She smacked Floyd in the shoulder.

"He's a carpenter! Come on!" Floyd defended himself as he smiled.

"Oh, you are?" Allison asked.

I laughed. "Yeah, it's just a joke gift."

"I guess that is pretty funny since you do woodworking," she laughed.

"Exactly," Chris said, coming over to me. "It's awesome. Floyd was a little apprehensive, but Levi and I talked him into getting it for you." He patted me on the shoulder.

"You know you like the keychain," Levi said, grinning.

I nodded. "It's kinda funny."

Levi stood up and said, "Okay, everyone... there's still one more gift left."

Floyd and Margret looked over to the tree. "No there isn't," they said at the same time.

"Everyone, leave your gifts behind and let's go for a

walk… This gift is for Mom and Dad or however you know them."

Levi led the family outside and across the gravel driveway towards the milk house. As we walked, the children were whispering amongst themselves on their speculation of what was going on. The adults kept the table gift away from the children in fear they might blurt it out before it was revealed. As we came to the corner of the milk house, Levi stopped and asked for Floyd and Margret to come up to the front of the group.

"We all know you two were married just a few days after Christmas, and this year we wanted to do something special for you. This is a Christmas and Anniversary present… From all of us kids and grandkids."

I felt extremely nervous as Levi spoke. There was a bit of fear with every piece of furniture I crafted, but this one especially. I had toiled so long on the table and chairs, trying to make sure every single piece was perfect… I'd be devastated if they didn't like it. And after my father's comment on the flaws, my nerves were unhinged in anticipation of everybody's reaction.

Levi looked up at the sky. "The snow seems to have stopped. Chris and Levi, could you come get it ready?"

"Sure," I replied, glancing back at the people to spot Chris near the back. I motioned with a nod to him to follow me. Chris and I undid the tie downs and pulled off the tarps, while leaving the blankets on.

Levi stuck his head around the corner of the milk house. "Ready for us?"

"Yep."

Everyone came around the corner and fixed their gaze on the blankets. More whispering came about by the children, then Levi interrupted. "Go ahead."

Chris and I nodded to each other and pulled off the blankets, revealing the table and chairs. My eyes bounced between Floyd and Margret as I searched their face for a response in their body language.

Floyd stepped out and walked up to the table. He walked around the table, looking at all the work that had gone into it. He shook his head as tears began to stream down his face. Then he stopped and looked over at Levi and then over at me.

"Simply amazing," Floyd said delicately. "This table is so beautifully crafted and even more stunning than the old one we used to have. You did this, Dylan? Without the help of Frank or anyone else?" He asked, stepping closer to me. Seeing a grown man cry wasn't something I saw very often and it warmed my heart to make such an impact on Floyd.

"Yes," I said softly glancing over at Levi. "It was all Levi's idea though."

Floyd stepped over to Levi and hugged him. "Thank you so much, Son!"

Margret joined Floyd's side. "We love it, and although it doesn't replace the old one that we lost in the fire, it will serve our family for generations to come. New memories will be made starting with this night. Thank you so much!" Margret said with tears streaming down her face. "Bring it inside, and we'll have tonight's meal served on it!"

Levi looked over at me and gave me a nod. Everything

went off without a hitch. They loved the table. As Levi, Chris, Craig, Jeremy and I all carried the new chairs and table inside and the old one out to the milk house, Levi kept smiling at me. He seemed thrilled with the result. As the table got set by Molly and Olivia back inside, Levi asked me to come out on the front porch.

"What's going on?" I asked, closing the door behind me.

"Thank you, Dylan. I can't believe how perfect the table turned out. It's better than any of us could have expected."

"It was my pleasure to help you out."

Levi pulled out a folded check from his coat pocket and handed it to me. "That's from all of us, for your time and our thankfulness."

"I can't take that," I said, slipping the folded check back into his pocket. "Just to see everyone happy is enough." I turned and began going back inside.

"You're a good man, Dylan," Levi said.

"I am but a man," I replied. "God's grace and love is what I want you to see when you look at me."

Levi nodded. "Well, you're doing a great job at that. Keep it up."

Coming back inside off the porch, the ham was being served on the new table waiting for memories to be made. That Christmas Eve, I sat with the Nortaggen's family and shared an evening of love, laughter and thankfulness that I'll never forget.

DECEMBER 31, 2010

Another record day of snowfall loomed over the big New Years Eve bash out at Roy's farm. Everyone was going. I even convinced my dad to join us for the celebration. He said he couldn't promise to stay until midnight, but he'd try his best to stay as long as he could.

Chris was buzzed before we even got out to the farm. His love for drinking was getting the best of him more every day. Just a few days ago I caught him downing vodka behind the Feed Store on his lunch break, putting his career at risk. When I confronted him about it, he shrugged it off and said it helps the slow times at work be a little less mundane. I didn't buy the story, but I wasn't sure exactly what I could do about it, either.

We arrived a little after six, just an hour before the party, to see if there was anything we could do to help. Approaching Levi out in the lower lofting shed that was attached to Roy's barn, I found him chopping wood, and I asked, "Need a hand with that?"

Levi looked confused at me as he checked his watch. "You're an hour early."

Nodding I replied, "I wanted to help."

He smiled and nodded, "I'll take the offer. Grab that wheelbarrow and push it up to the front of the house. Just stack the wood out on the patio near the back door."

"Alright," I replied. Stopping before I grabbed the wheelbarrow, I asked, "Random question here, but what's up with Allison? She married?"

"She was…" Levi replied.

"Okay…"

"She's a nice gal and all, but she's going through a tough spot right now. I don't know if she really wants to be with anyone."

"I wasn't thinking that, just curious," I replied. Grabbing onto each handle, I lifted up the wheelbarrow handles and wheeled it up to the back patio in front of the farmhouse. As I stacked the wood along the side of the house, I could see through the curtains and into the living room. Allison was removing pictures from the wall behind the television. Those pictures had been there ever since I met Roy and I was startled to see her pulling them off the wall.

Coming in through the patio door quickly, I asked, "What are you doing?"

"Don't worry," Roy said, coming in from the dining room. "She's doing a little redecorating."

"Oh…" I replied, relaxing my composure. "I didn't realize that."

"Ally was an interior designer back in Atlanta and I asked what she could do with a few rooms in the house."

Jess came in from the kitchen. "Those pictures," she paused for a moment as she finished her strawberry. "And this entire house hasn't changed since I was just a little kid."

Roy smiled over at Jess and said, "And we just want a little change and freshness here for the babies when they arrive. She's already almost finished with the nursery."

"Nursery?" I asked.

"Want to see it?" Jess asked hopefully, clearly wanting to show off her new babies' room.

Glancing back out the windows to the patio, I said, "Sure. I'll take a look really quick."

Following Jess, I went upstairs and into the room across from her and Levi's. Opening the door, I saw half the room was in light grey and a soft pink while the other side was in a baby blue and a light grey. A few furniture boxes sat against the wall. "Wow, that's a really cool design on the walls."

"I know, I love it," Jess replied. "The cribs and dresser is all solid white. It'll look perfect. It worked out pretty nicely that Henry just left for college right before the pregnancy happened."

"How is Henry anyway? I'm surprised he wasn't here for Christmas."

"He's good. He was with his girlfriend. He's super involved with her and decided to visit her family instead of coming here for the holidays."

"I see," I replied. "So… Allison… She was married?" I asked.

"Yeah she was married, but the guy was a jerk and it didn't work out. She needed to get away from the city life; that's why she came here. Why? Are you interested in her Dylan?" She was smiling.

"No, well… she's cute. I don't really know her though. She seems nice," I replied.

"Yeah, she's really awesome; so talented. She is not even charging us half what she did in Atlanta for her clients too." Jess informed me as she twirled around the nursery ecstatically.

She's charging? For family? Seriously? I have no room to judge her. She is a professional and owns her own business after all, but wow, don't know what to think about that one. But it wasn't any of my business to bring up my concern with Jess. "Well, that's nice of her," I replied as we exited to go back downstairs. "When's she going back to Atlanta?"

"She probably isn't," Jess replied as we continued down the stairs.

"Is she staying with you guys long term?"

"No, she and the kids will probably be out in the spring, around the same time the twins come. I don't know for sure, though."

"I see," I replied.

Coming back into the living room, I said, "That nursery looks awesome, Allison."

"Thanks," Allison said as she finished taking the last picture down behind the television. "The nursery was inspired by one of the women's Bible Study leaders at my church in Atlanta. When I saw her baby's nursery, I took pictures for a future project. It turned out to be this one!"

I smiled. "That's neat you can be inspired by other sources of work. Well, I better get back outside. I'm helping Levi with the wood and he's probably wondering where I'm at."

Going back outside, I found Sammy sitting inside my wheelbarrow. "Did you need a ride, sir?" I asked grinning.

He said nothing and just nodded his head a little bit.

"Please keep all hands, feet and other body parts inside the wheelbarrow at all times. Be sure to securely hold onto each side of the wheelbarrow during the duration of your travel. And oh, thank you for choosing Holden Airways."

Zooming through the front yard through the snow, I pushed as we crossed the deep snow. Growing weary before making it to the sidewalk, I said, "Please be understanding of the slight delay, for we have hit some severe weather and will be traveling a bit slower for a moment."

Sammy laughed as he jumped a little in his seat. "C'mon, c'mon," he shouted from the wheelbarrow. I made it to the sidewalk where it was clear and continued a quicker pace out to the lower lofting shed.

As I slowed down to the wood pile where Levi was standing with Chris, I said, "Thank you again for traveling with Holden Airways, please have a wonderful night and a happy new year."

Sammy climbed out of the wheelbarrow and ran off to meet up with his sister Olivia, who looked to be jealously standing nearby at the loft's entrance. Chris and Levi watched as they ran off behind me. Taking off my jacket, I wiped my forehead of sweat as I took a deep breath.

"You're sure good with kids," Levi said.

Nodding, I replied, "Kids are a lot more fun than adults."

Chris laughed, "I'm having fun, Bro!"

"You're just drunk…" I said, not amused.

Chris came up to me. "I'm having fun." His tone was sharp. If it wasn't for the fact my father was soon arriving, I would have pushed him back right then, but I didn't want a fight to break out and cause a scene as my dad showed up.

"Get out of my face," I laughed.

"Chris… you start fighting, you're gone," Levi interjected. "Jess told me if you even show up buzzing too strongly, she wants me to make you leave. So just cool it."

"I'm good," Chris said, backing away. He left the shed.

"I saw the way you looked at Ally the other day on Christmas Eve, and now you're asking about her more... I want to warn you, she's not someone you want to be with, probably," Levi said, loading another block up on the chopping block.

Glancing towards the farmhouse, I said, "How come you say that?"

"She talks an awful lot about the kids' Dad, Adam. I don't know if that whole thing is over between them."

"You said they got a divorce."

"That doesn't mean he died. Their dad will forever be in the picture, forever. They were a family for years, that doesn't just disappear when some papers are signed. That's something you got to realize. Just try to be careful buddy. I care about you and just don't want you to get hurt. That's all I want to say about it."

"I'll keep that in mind," I replied as I began picking up more blocks of firewood. "I take it we're doing a bonfire in the yard?"

"You know it," Levi grinned. "Jess picked up s'mores supplies today in town also, so that should be fun."

"I love those things..."

"I know, right?" Levi replied. "I can't wait until my kids are here and then I get to teach them to roast marshmallows."

Nodding, I said, "It'll be a bit before they are old enough to get it... But that'll be pretty cool."

"Did you know Ally's never had a s'more?" Levi asked.

"What? I don't believe it."

"Yep, she's never even heard of them before."

"Bizarre. Maybe she isn't right for me," I replied laughing.

Levi laughed.

Later that evening, I sat down next to my father at the bonfire. "Dad," I said with a nod as I loaded my marshmallow up on the end of my poker.

"Son," he replied. Turning to me, he continued, "I spoke a little with Levi earlier inside after dinner. He said Floyd and all the family was quite impressed with the table. He passed a message along from Floyd saying thank you for raising such a wonderful young man."

I nodded.

"I want you to know son, even if I don't talk about how great you are or pat you on the back when you do something, that doesn't mean it goes unnoticed."

"Thanks Dad," I replied. He was trying, and I appreciated the effort he was attempting to show towards me. Maybe being on the brink of death was making him relax a little more in life. I didn't want to think about him dying. Even if he was a jerk for all these years, I didn't want my dad to be gone. I needed to prove to him I was capable and deserving of his love and approval. I wanted to run the inn and show him I could do it and make him proud.

Pushing my poker into the fire, just above the flames, I slowly turned it as the marshmallow browned.

Olivia's marshmallow caught fire and she pulled it out quickly. "Dang it, again!" She said with a sigh.

My father looked at her and I saw him do something he didn't do very often; he put someone else before himself. "Let me help you get the perfect marshmallow. Can I do that?"

She agreed with a nod and handed him the poker. Loading a fresh marshmallow up on the end, he held it above the flame as he explained the reason and how to roast a proper marshmallow. "Slowly cooking it takes more time, but it melts the insides just right and results in the perfect s'more."

Grinning as she took the poker, she said, "Like this?"

He lifted part of the poker closest to her up. "Just a smidge higher above the flames; you get too close and it'll ignite again."

"What's ignite?" she asked.

"I meant catch on fire," He replied with a warm smile. This man that I called my father was acting like an entirely different person and I loved every moment of it. I said a quick prayer thanking God for the change.

Sitting back, he watched as Olivia cooked the marshmallow over the open flame and I saw something happen again in my father I wasn't used to seeing, he smiled genuinely.

His smile drew out my concern I had for his life. I knew it was fragile and delicate; I needed to know more than the simple fact he wasn't going to be around much longer, so I tried asking. "How's everything going for you? With your health and all?"

"It's okay son," he replied patting my leg. "Starting here in a week or so, Lenny will be taking over the inn. I spoke with him about having you help with the renovations; he agreed quickly. He said he will give you a buzz when he needs you. I'll still be living at the inn and helping with what I can."

"Great," I replied, a little dismayed. He answered my question like a politician does, sidestepping and saying words without actually answering the question. I wanted to know everything I could possibly.

"I see your brother isn't improving much," Frank said as he fixed his eyes on Chris over at the tree in the front yard. He was leaned over and vomiting.

"He's fighting less… so that's some progress," I replied.

"I suppose. And you haven't been joining him?"

"No sir," I replied confidently. "I won't be sucked into that garbage again."

"Atta boy," Frank said. "Well, it's just about nine and I'm feeling rather tired. I'll see you around." He began to stand up and I helped him.

"Could I come by the inn and see you sometime?" I asked.

"Sure," He replied smiling.

"We missed you on Christmas… We even tried calling you," I said.

"Yeah, I had a bad day on that particular day… Sometimes I'm just too weak to even get up in the morning," He replied, appearing to be a little shocked at himself for the over share of information.

"Do you need me to come stay with you?" I asked.

"No son, I can handle myself," he replied. He was stubborn and unrelenting in his insatiable need to be independent.

Walking with him out to his truck, I thought about how there wouldn't be too many more goodbyes until the big one. As he backed out, I waved at him and smiled. Another wave of sadness came over me and my eyes began to water a little.

Interrupting my thoughts, Allison startled me from behind. "Dylan."

Jumping, I turned and snapped, "What?" Wiping my eyes quickly as I bent over, I said, "It's kind of dusty out here."

"Really?" Ally said glancing back towards the bonfire in the yard for a moment. "You don't have to lie to kick it. The ground is covered in snow. Anyways, I was just going to see if you wanted another s'more."

I went red in embarrassment. "I'm alright. Thanks Allison."

"No worries. You can call me Ally though. Only people I don't like call me Allison."

I laughed. "That's a strange quirk."

Shrugging, she replied, "It's my way of reminding myself who I don't like."

"I'm glad I made the good list," I replied. "You enjoying it out at Roy's?"

Turning as we walked back to the bonfire, she nodded. "It's really nice to be back in a Christian environment."

"What do you mean?"

Stopping she looked at me. "The city is oversaturated with liberal-minded people; it's a different culture all together versus a place like Chattaroy. I love being out here with people who share my own beliefs." She looked over at Jess who was motioning her over. "I'll see you around; I'm being beckoned." She smiled and headed over to Jess.

"Duuuuuuuudeeeeee………." Chris said swinging his arm around my shoulder. "Tap that."

"Don't act like a teenager," I replied, pushing his arm off.

"Stop being a prude!" He replied.

Ignoring his comment, I asked, "Where's Elly? Shouldn't she be here by now?"

"Roy said she called from work and left a message on the answering machine inside. She said she got stuck and had to stay late. She wasn't going to make it."

"Dang," I replied. "Sorry to hear about it."

"Whatever; just means she won't be nagging me to slow down on the drinking."

Shaking my head, I replied, "I will still be here."

His drinking was getting worse and I suspected that might have been a reason for Elly's lack of involvement in tonight's festivities. It was beginning to become more problematic for him with every passing day and I worried about my brother's future.

JANUARY 14, 2011

As I was shutting off the lathe in the shop, the phone began ringing above my workbench. Glancing over at the clock I saw it was only seven o'clock in the morning. Who could be calling this early? I wondered as I dusted off my shirt of the sawdust to go answer the phone.

"Hey Dylan, it's your uncle Lenny," a voice on the other end of the phone said.

"Oh, hey Lenny. What's up?"

"Can you come down to the inn? I want to sit down and discuss your involvement moving forward with the renovations."

"Sure, when?" I asked.

"What's a good time for you? I'll be here all day."

Glancing at the clock, I knew I needed to drop off the table I already made down at the feed store before they opened at nine. "I need to run an errand, but I can be there later in the morning, probably somewhere around eleven or so."

"Sounds good," He replied as he paused for a moment. "Your Dad wanted me to see if he could get you to bring an old photo album of his..."

"Which one? He has a few boxes of stuff over here," I replied glancing over to the corner of the shop where they were.

"The one with pictures of your Mother."

Nodding, I replied, "I'll bring it."

Hanging up with Lenny, I ventured over to the boxes. My father had me take the boxes after Chris and I got into our own place. He said there wasn't room at the inn, but I think he just wanted us to hold onto to some stuff in case of a fire. He was kind of paranoid of fires, ever since we were just kids.

Opening up one of the dusty boxes, I straightway spotted my old baseball glove. Picking it up, I blew the dust off and slid my fingers in. My mind jumped back in time to when Chris and I were younger, I was but twelve years of age. It was the one time in life that we both were able to play on the same sports team, the Chattaroy Bobcats. I played shortstop while Chris played left field. I could still smell the freshly cut grass in the football fields just west of where we practiced. Breaking through my thoughts, Chris came into the shop.

"Who was on the phone?" he asked, coming over to me as I stood over the box. "Why are you in Dad's boxes?"

"It was Lenny; Dad wants the photo album with Mom."

"I see," He replied softly. "Sure would have been nice if we could have gotten to know her before she died."

"Yeah," I replied, looking down. "I bet she was amazing, just like Dad always describes her."

He nodded. Spotting my glove on, Chris began to smile. "I sure miss tossing the ball around out in the back of the inn, dude."

Smiling back at him, I nodded. "Remember when you broke Mrs. Bovey's cabin window out?" I began laughing.

"How could I forget? Dad was so pissed he threw the baseball into the lake, losing it forever."

I laughed again as I pulled the glove off and tossed it back into the box. "Those were the days…"

"They were great," he replied smiling.

Noticing Chris's name tag, I noticed 'assistant manager' under his name. "When did that happen?"

"What?" He asked.

"Assistant Manager? You have it on your name tag."

"Last night," He replied. "You had already crashed out by the time Ken dropped me off."

"That's great, Bro!" I said.

"Yep, and Ken has an old car he doesn't use. He's selling it to me for only a few hundred dollars. I'm going to get it tonight when I get off work."

"Awesome!"

"Yeah," He let out a relieved breath of air as he continued smiling. "No more two thirty to close shifts for me!"

"Sweet," I replied. "I'm happy for you. You are opening today, then?"

"Yeah."

"I'll give you a ride into work. I need to take that table I finished up in anyways."

"Okay," He replied.

Turning back to the box, I began digging around inside of it in search of the photo album. Bypassing all the memorabilia from our childhood, I found the pink photo album. Pulling it out, I wiped it off and cracked it open.

Seeing a young picture of my mother and father on the first page, I smiled. My memory of her is fragmented and I suspect many of the memories I have are just made up from the stories our father would tell us mingled with looking at the pictures of her so many times. Pictures often have a funny way of telling a much different story than the reality of what happened. I find that people often smile in photographs and they are usually doing something fun, like a vacation, barbeque with friends and so on. While my mother smiled in every photo we had of her, hidden behind that smile was a battle she fought every day. There were no photos of her screaming in the middle of the night because of nightmares that terrorized her or the locking of herself in the bathroom with a bottle of vodka. Those weren't memories you'd find in a photograph; they were tucked away in the minds of those who knew her best, hidden away from the world. My father told us she fought depression up until she finally died. My father didn't like talking about the darker days; he tried to always remind us of the good days he shared with her.

Chris joined me in my gaze at our parents together in the picture and said, "I'm glad I don't remember her. Those last days before she died were terrible... at least according to Dad. It'd be hard to have those memories to deal with."

"Yeah, I couldn't imagine," I replied with a softened tone.

Pointing to the picture we were both looking at, Chris smiled, "I'd rather have these pictures of her happy anyways."

I nodded. "Me too."

Chris helped me with unloading the table and chairs at the feed store right out front. Once Ken saw us from inside, he came outside to greet us.

"You're getting better with every piece of furniture you make," Ken said as he admired the cherry finish on the table. I had used the leftovers I had from Floyd's table.

"Thanks," I replied.

"How's your Dad doing?" Ken asked.

"I haven't seen him in a couple weeks, but he seemed fine when I saw him holding on."

"Chris here was saying he was at that thing out at Roy's for the New Year's celebration, that's good he got out and about."

"Yeah, and he seemed coherent and whatnot... So I don't know. Guess I'll find out today, I'm heading out there now."

Ken nodded as he shook my hand. "Thanks for another beautiful piece of furniture. Tell your Dad I said hello."

"I'll let him know," I replied, smiling. Noticing the rocking chair that was outside on the store's front entrance was gone, I asked, "My rocking chair sold?"

"Yep, sure did. I haven't cut you a check for it, but you can probably pick it up this afternoon."

Shaking my head, I replied, "Just give it to Chris and he can bring it home with him."

Getting back into my truck, I waved to Chris and Ken and headed towards the Silverback.

The inn was located along the lake that was on the outer skirts of Chattaroy. A hidden gem tucked away in the countryside where you could hear the sound of your own footsteps on the dozens of walking paths around the lake. The Silverback Inn wasn't your typical hotel. It consisted of multiple cabins independent from one another. Many of the cabins had balconies off the back that overlooked the lake. The Silverback Inn was an amazing place to just get away from the busyness of life and unwind.

Arriving at the inn, I pulled in, passing the sign that my father had crafted from an old oak tree that blew over in a storm some twenty years ago. Crossing over the bridge and under the draping snow-covered willow trees that shaded the pathway up to the office, I recalled my childhood and the races my brother Chris and I would have from the bridge up to the office. He never once could beat me, and it drove him nuts, since he was the one that was in track and field in high school. I smiled as I saw my father out shoveling snow just outside the front office. I was relieved to see him outside working; it gave me hope that he still had a while to live.

Pulling right up to him, I parked and got out of my truck. Turning, he smiled at me and I was again caught off guard by his warm embrace. It just wasn't like him. As I approached, I said, "You sure been smiling a lot lately."

He came closer and hugged me. "There's a lot to smile about son." He turned back to the shovel and began pushing snow again as he continued talking, "I've been talking with Pastor Johnny over at the church about God…"

"Wow." My father, the devote atheist, was in talks with the pastor? Could my ears be deceiving me or was my lifelong prayer finally being answered? I cannot recall how many nights I found myself troubled and unable to sleep while I thought of his and my brother's eternal destinations. I broke into a large grin across my face.

"Yes. I know it's hard to believe son, but last week, I gave my heart to Jesus." He had a grin from ear to ear as he sighed with relief. I smiled back at him.

Elated, I asked "How did this happen?"

"Well, I've been meeting with the Pastor for a couple months now. Ever since I found out I wasn't going to live much longer, I just had that question you asked me a long time ago stuck in my head."

"What question?" I asked curiously.

"What happens when you die, Daddy? You asked me that years and years ago."

Shaking my head, I said, "I don't remember asking that, but I'm glad I did." Giving him a hug I continued, "I'm so happy you made that commitment to Christ, Dad."

"So am I, the baptism is the week after next."

"How the heck are you, Dylan?" Lenny asked coming out of the front office with a big silly grin on his face. He was a scrawny guy with straggly brown hair and a five o'clock shadow. I hadn't seen him in years, but he didn't look like he had aged a day.

"I'm good Lenny... How are you?"

Coming up to me, he shook my hand and replied, "I'm great, man. Don't you just love this place?"

"Beats Wenatchee?"

"Sure does... Glad your Dad had me come down."

Glancing over at my dad, he continued, "Mind if I steal your boy for a moment to talk some business?"

My dad shook his head, "Not at all. I best get back to moving this snow."

Lenny and I went into the office and took a seat at the desk up front, just inside the door.

As I took a seat, I asked, "How long have you been at the helm?"

Smiling, he sat down in the chair behind the desk. "It's still your Dad's place right now. It's all just in a transitional period."

"I see," I replied.

"Your Dad's been doing this all his life… I figured it'd take some transitioning for him to get used to not being in control." His eyes shifted over to the window for a moment as he continued. "As you can see, he's still trying to be actively involved."

"I saw that," I replied. "Dad's being vague about his condition… do you know any of the details?" I asked as I glanced over my shoulder towards my father outside.

Shaking his head, he replied, "Nope… I tried prying it out of him, but he's been pretty closed-lipped about it."

"You think he's going to be around for a while?" I asked.

He nodded. "I wouldn't worry too much about him, Dylan. So Frank said he told you about the improvements we're doing?"

"He did, but he didn't go into a whole bunch of detail."

"Basically, the way I see it." He leaned over the desk as his tone got more serious. "The Silverback is a gold mine for tourists, but it's so far off the beaten path that most people don't even know about it." His voice got a little quieter. "I took a look at the financials a while back and they are okay, but we need to bring it up and I think we can."

"With remodeling and updating?"

"Yes, but also with some marketing. We need to get the Silverback name out there. We don't have a website, no ads, no nothing. It's purely word of mouth right now. I think I did catch a lone review online somewhere, but the point is we got a lot of work ahead of us."

"I'm not big on the whole internet thing. I wouldn't be much help on that."

"And that's fine. I have a guy I'm working with on that. I'll show you what I need from you," he replied, smiling as he stood up. He led me out to the cabins as he continued talking. "The furniture your father made in all these units was amazing… back in the eighties, but it's outdated and breaking apart now."

We came up to one of the cabins and he unlocked the door, letting me go inside first. He said over my shoulder, "See that bed?"

"Yeah," I replied looking at the sleigh bed that sat against the cabin wall.

"Gorgeous bed, but check this out," He replied passing me and pointing to the side of the bed. Coming over to it,

I saw a big chunk missing out of the wood.

"How's that even happen?" I asked curiously.

"I don't really know, but there's little issues like this all over in the units. Dressers, TV stands, tables and the bed frames. Instead of just fixing them I would rather just update and redo everything to bring life back into this place."

"What are you thinking on the beds? Make a bunch of new sleigh beds?"

"Well, that or save a little on cost and just make new and simple wood bed frames."

"Stain or paint?"

"I don't know yet."

"Stain would probably keep the rustic feel of the rooms."

"That's true," he replied with a nod. Looking me over, he asked, "So, you up for it?"

"For sure, whatever I can do to help," I replied.

"You'll be compensated for your time since you wouldn't be able to make furniture for the feed store anymore."

Nodding, I replied, "Okay, I'm cool with that."

We shook on it. I felt good about Lenny taking over for my father until I proved myself worthy. He was a good man and had the Holden's best interest in mind, and knew way more about marketing and everything else that went into running an entire business. Working on furniture for the inn was a dream I'd had in the back of my mind ever since I started woodworking. Lenny was going to make that dream a reality for me and I was going to be able to make my dad proud. This was going to be good for all of us.

JANUARY 25, 2011

Two days ago, my father was baptized down at Chattaroy Baptist. His profession of faith before the small congregation was heartfelt and moving. I had dreamt of the day ever since I came to the saving knowledge of Christ myself as a young man. I slipped into the back of the crowd that day to catch the baptism and left before anyone in the congregation noticed I was even there. I did however make eye contact with my father and the pastor. My father beamed at me while the pastor gave me a look that felt like a fire and brimstone sermon in the mere five seconds we made eye contact. I knew it was about my lack of church attendance. I didn't feel like I could go to church. I was extremely busy working endlessly and trying to stock up furniture at the feed store before starting in on the big Silverback Inn project. I barely had time to eat, let alone peel myself away for a few hours on Sundays.

After getting back home from the baptism of my father that Sunday, I finished up the final pieces of furniture I promised to do for the feed store. I had to make sure Ken was taken care of with enough stock while I was working for Lenny. On Monday, I dropped off the furniture to the feed store and started that evening on the Silverback's first project task, which was an order for ten tables.

Taking a break out in the shop late Tuesday afternoon, I wiped the sweat from my brow and thought about the fact I hadn't seen much of Chris lately. Going into the house, I found Chris napping on the couch with the TV blaring. Picking up the remote, I shut it off and it somehow startled him awake.

"I was watching that," he said, sitting up on the couch.

"I'm sure you were, Bro. Do wanna go eat at the Wagon Wheel?" I asked as he stretched.

"Sure," he said. Looking around as he seemed to gather his thoughts, he reached beside the couch and pulled out a bottle of whiskey.

"You been drinking all day?" I asked concerned.

"It's my day off... just trying to relax, dude. Chill."

Shaking my head, I said, "There's relaxing and then there is being an alcoholic."

"You think I'm an alcoholic because I drink a couple times a week? Come off it."

"Come off what? I think it's a problem when you need

to drink. Or you set up specific days to be drinking…"

"Well I don't need it, I just want it." He laughed, standing up. He shook my shoulder. "Don't worry about me, Bro. I got this."

I wanted to tell him how he was going to get left out of ownership of the inn if he didn't stop drinking, but I didn't want to do that to my dad; he was trusting me. My father wanted the same as I did for Chris. We wanted him to stop drinking on his own without a financial gain attached to it. We both knew if he could stop on his own without being rewarded he'd likely be able to stick with it in the long term. "Whatever," I replied, heading for the front door.

Coming off the steps on the way out to the truck, Chris slipped and hit his head against the porch. "Ouch!" He yelled as he grabbed his head.

Glancing back at him, I shook my head.

"Shut up, it was ice." He stood back up and continued past me on the way to my truck. Looking back at the steps, shaking my head I saw there was no ice. He was just drunk and missed a step. I said a prayer for his safety.

Getting over to the Wagon Wheel, we were greeted by Trisha. "How's it going, Dylan? Haven't seen much of you here with your brother."

"Yeah, I don't come down here much anymore. Been busy and whatnot," I replied.

"He doesn't keep his protective eye on me anymore," Chris added. "He finally let me be a big boy all on my own." His mocking tone was agitating me, but I pushed it aside.

"Could we just get a table, in the dining area?" I asked.

"Sure," she replied. We followed Trisha over to a booth in the dining area and we took our seats. Chris asked her, "We still on for later tonight?"

"Yeah," she replied, smiling before she left our table back to the front.

Confused, I asked, "What's going on with you and her tonight?"

"We're meeting a few over at Copper's Cove to toss a couple back."

"How's Elly feel about that?" I asked.

"She and I are done, dude." Chris folded his hands. "She broke up with me a week ago."

"What? Why didn't you say anything?"

He shrugged. "Didn't see it as a big deal." He was lying. I knew Chris better than I knew anyone else on this planet and he was upset. He was just hiding it behind his macho persona.

"You're my brother and Elly's my friend, it's a big deal."

"Well, it's been a week and you didn't know about it... so I guess you aren't that great of friends with her."

Chris's attitude was wearing thin on my nerves. I was working endlessly trying to help Dad with the inn and help kindle the relationship I missed with him growing up and Chris still hadn't even been to visit him once. My resentment towards my brother was building, but I prayed for God to help me and He did.

Curious, I asked, "Why won't you go see Dad, Bro?"

"That's out of left field… But if I went out there, what would I even say?" He asked.

"I don't know… but you know he's dying and-"

Chris interrupted me. "Wait a minute, wait a minute… You mean to tell me because the guy is dying that I need to go visit him? After everything he has put us through?"

"Dad's going to die, Chris."

"So?"

"That's harsh…"

"No it's not, Dylan! It wasn't too long ago you were checking out our front window to see if he brought his gun and now you are bugging at me about seeing him… I just don't get it."

"We might never have another chance on this earth to see him… I'd hate for you to have regret after he does kick the bucket."

"He's hurt me, hurt us, far too much in this life to just forget about it and move on like nothing ever happened. I can't just forgive and forget like that."

"I am forgiving, but I'm not forgetting, Chris. I love Dad, despite the way he chose to treat us. People need second chances…"

Shaking his head, he looked at me with narrowed eyes, "I think he's faking it, Dylan. I don't think he's dying. You talk about how good he's doing and all this… it just irks me."

"He got saved a few weeks ago, he's doing better, Brother. Ill or not, he's a different guy," I replied.

"Whatever. I'll see if the change sticks before I start going out of my way to see him. And if he's not really dying, that'd be messed up."

"I know it's hard, Bro. But he isn't lying. I talked to Lenny, he's in charge now. It's real." The server came over; it was Elly. Awkward silence filled the air for a moment before I broke it. "Hey, Elly… Surprised you didn't have someone else fill in for our table."

"Unfortunately, nobody else is available at the moment to take your table. This is a rather small town, ya know…"

"I see… In that case, I'll take water to drink."

"And a pitcher of beer for Chris, got it." She stormed off from the table.

"Woah…" I said watching her leave. "You got her pretty upset, eh?"

"Yeah, she thinks I have a drinking problem…"

Nodding, I smiled. "Weird, don't know why she'd think that."

"Whatever. I'm sick of you and everyone else trying to tell me what I'm doing wrong in my life!" He snapped at me.

"That was abrupt."

"I'm just tired of it…" Chris leaned across the table, and said, "Even if I drink a little more than I should, how's that hurting anyone? I don't drive when I drink and I keep my cool."

"Fighting is not keeping your cool."

Shaking his head, he said, "Fighting only happens when people stick their nose where it doesn't belong or say something they shouldn't. You remember that last fight me and you were in? Those guys were insulting us, and on purpose!" He laughed as he continued shaking his head. "I don't pick fights, they just… happen, ya know? Gotta right the wrong in the world."

Nodding, I was done trying to talk any real sense into him. "Okay." He relaxed back into his seat and seemed to take note of my annoyance with him. Trying to lighten the tension I sensed between us, I asked, "How's the assistant manager gig going?"

"It's good. Haven't done a whole lot, I did handle a customer complaint the other day about our windows having streaks on them from the glass cleaner."

I laughed. "Really? What'd they say? Who was it?"

He smiled. "It was Polly, from down the road from us. She said that she could see the streaks and that business would probably pick up if we kept the windows in nicer condition."

I laughed. "She's so nitpicky."

"I know," Chris replied. "I assured her we would get on it. Then I had Tyler go clean the windows when he got in that afternoon."

"That's awesome," I replied. Chris smiled and nodded.

Elly came back for another round of awkwardness and took our orders. She was cold the entire time, even to me. After our meal, Chris elected to stay behind and watch the game on the TV in the bar.

"I'm going to take off," I said as I walked with Chris towards the bar section of the restaurant. "How are you meeting up with Trisha? You came with me. You got a ride?"

"I'll just watch the game until she gets off and hitch a ride with her."

"Okay," I replied. "Have a safe night."

Chris nodded back to me as he turned and went into the bar. I worried about him and I wanted to find out if there was more to the story between him and Elly. I knew Jess and Elly were best friends so I headed towards Roy's place to go find out the truth.

Arriving out at Roy's, it was just after seven o'clock that evening. I was heading up the sidewalk when I heard a faint whimper from over near the hillside that led down to the creek. Cutting through the lawn I came over to the hill to see it was Sammy sitting on a ball of snow.

"What's going on Sammy?" I asked, bending a knee to meet him at eye level. The light pole in the front yard didn't stretch over to the hill, but the glow from the house helped to see him slightly through the darkness of the evening.

"Liv wouldn't help me build a snowman."

"Sounds rough," I replied with a nod. "Why don't you just wait for tomorrow when it's light out?"

"I want to build a snowman now."

"Sometimes you don't get what you want."

"Why not?"

"You can't make people do what you want." His cheeks looked rosy red from being outside in the chilly wintery air. "Come inside and warm up."

"I want to build a snowman!"

"Tell you what, why don't you come inside with me and I'll do that magic coin trick for you."

Sammy smiled. "Okay." He hopped off the ball of snow and we headed into the porch. Helping him out of his snow suit, we went into the kitchen where Jess and Levi were sitting at the table. He must have forgotten about the coin trick as he darted through the kitchen and headed off to the living room.

"Hi, Dylan," Jess said from the kitchen table.

"Those babies look like they're about to come out!" I replied.

She rubbed her belly and smiled. "I'm ready for them to!"

"What brings you out?" Levi asked as he took a drink of his coffee.

Taking a seat at the table, I sighed. "My brother. I'm getting worried about his drinking."

"It seems to be worse lately," Jess said.

"I know, it sucks..." I paused for a moment as I chose my words. "Did Elly talk to you about what happened between them?"

"Yeah, she said his drinking just got to a point where she couldn't deal with it anymore. He's not even the Chris she remembers..."

Nodding, I replied, "That's kind of what Chris said. Did something happen?"

Jess looked over at Levi and he sighed. "Tell him," Levi said to her with a nod.

Jess narrowed her gaze at me. "Do you know how bad his drinking is?"

"I know he's drinking a lot on days off."

She shook her head. "He's always drunk. Literally from the moment he wakes up and until he goes to bed. He even wakes up in the night to take swigs. Elly said it's horrible... He needs help, Dylan."

"Wow, I guess I didn't know the extent."

"He's even drinking while he's working..." she said softly. "He's going to drink himself to death if something doesn't change."

The phone suddenly rang, pulling Jess away from the kitchen. Levi leaned his arms on the table and said, "I'm sorry about your brother. Wish there was something one of us could do. We've been keeping him in our prayers."

Nodding, I thought about it. "Thank you. I'm going to tell him he has to move out."

"He doesn't pay rent?" Levi asked.

"He owns it with me, but if I tell him I'm buying him out of his portion and want him gone, he'll leave from the awkwardness of the situation."

"You really think he'll leave? If he owns part of it with you?"

Nodding, I said, "I know my brother. He won't be comfortable being around. He'll move out."

Levi nodded. "Well it might be best if he left."

Jess came in from the other room. "Dylan…" Her voice was shaky and she had a fearful look in her eyes. "You need to go down to the Wagon Wheel…"

"What's wrong?" I asked.

"It's Chris. He's fighting."

Shaking my head, I said, "No. He needs to figure this out on his own."

"It's not like that this time. A group of gnarly looking dudes just took him out to the parking lot and Missy ain't there. Elly's worried."

"You should go," Levi said.

Coming into the kitchen, Sammy asked, "Can you show me the coin trick?" as I rose to my feet.

I bent a knee and smiled at him as I retrieved the wooden coin. Sliding it behind his head, I let it slide down my jacket sleeve and revealed it was gone. He smiled. Rubbing his head of hair, I said, "I'll teach it to you some day."

"Promise?" he asked as I stood up.

"Yeah," I replied. Looking to Jess and Levi, I said, "I'll go down there and get him. I'm going to give him an ultimatum tonight. Get his act together or move out."

"It's for the best," Levi said.

"You're going to just let him go live on the streets?" Jess asked worried.

"He has a job; he won't be on the street." Opening the porch door I said, "Thanks for the talk."

Looking up at the kitchen entrance, I saw Ally walking in from the dining room. "What's wrong?" she asked with a concerned look as she must have been able to read my demeanor.

"Chris got in another fight," I replied exasperated. "This time it's pretty bad sounding. I gotta go."

"Take care," Levi said from his chair.

"Hope everything turns out okay," Ally added.

"Thanks."

On the drive back to the Wagon Wheel, I thought

about Chris and his drinking. Where did it start? Why? And how come it was getting so frequent and out of control? These questions flooded my mind on the way to the Wagon Wheel.

As I arrived in the parking lot, I saw Chris with his arms being held behind his back by two familiar faces, but I couldn't place them immediately. His face was bloodied and his head was limp. My pulse quickened as I worried if he was dead or passed out. Then the guy who appeared to be taking shots at him turned to look at me as I pulled my truck right up behind them. It was the guy from a while back that called us hicks. It seemed he came back to settle the matter.

Leaping out of my truck without even turning it off, I stormed the group with my arm cocked back. I landed a blow to the guy's face, and he staggered backwards. Hearing footsteps behind me, I threw my elbow back, landing a blow to another dude's face and causing his nose to instantly begin to gush blood.

Turning around to the guys holding my brother, I ran up to them and pushed them off Chris. They both let go of him, causing him to fall to the pavement. I was able to grab onto one of the guys and shove him to the pavement but the other one landed a heavy blow to my side causing an instant sharp pain to rip through my torso. Swinging my arm around, I was able to connect a blow to his head and cause him to back away. Seeing a different guy grab Chris and just pull him up by his shirt slightly to take a cheap shot to his face, I surged with anger as I charged over to him. Yanking on his shoulder to pull him around to me, I exploded a punch into the guy's face. He fell backwards and hit the back of his head against the front bumper of a truck, causing him to be knocked out.

Trying to help Chris up to his feet, suddenly a hand on my shoulder pulled me around and it was the big nasty guy who called us hicks. He punched me right square in the face and then everything went dark.

FEBRUARY 10, 2011

With my doctor signing off on my ability to return to my normal activities, I walked out of the doctor's office feeling like a new man. My ribs were all healed up and I could finally return to making more furniture for the inn.

Getting home that afternoon, I was surprised to find Chris wasn't home. His car was missing out of the driveway but I knew it was his day off. That's strange, he's not home drinking… Maybe he decided to do something with his spare time other than drink? Shrugging it off, I went into the house and found the entire place trashed. The TV was knocked over, a lamp was smashed and the kitchen table was even flipped upside down. I was puzzled. What happened? Grabbing the phone from the kitchen wall, I began dialing the police to report a break in and then I saw Chris' baseball glove sitting on the couch. Hanging up the phone, I walked over and picked it up. I looked around and saw a few pictures from the boxes from dad, they were all crumpled up between the recliner and the couch. My pulse began racing as I wondered was my father... dead? I pushed the thought away quickly. Maybe Chris just went to go see him at the inn.

Running back into the kitchen, I checked the voicemails. There was one from Lenny. It felt like my heart stopped as he began to speak. His voice was broken and his words were strained.

"Hey kiddos. I got some bad news about your Dad..." He paused for a moment as he sniffled. "He's... in a better place now. He went during the night last night." Lenny began crying into the phone.

Shaking my head as I hung up, I rubbed the bridge of my nose with my index and thumb. "Why on earth would he leave that in a voicemail?" Turning, I looked back at the baseball glove and crumpled pictures as tears swelled in my eyes. Where is my brother? I walked out onto the front porch in shock of all that had transpired. Glancing across the street at the fields of snow and ice, I couldn't help but keep wondering where my brother could be. Sitting down on the bench up on our front porch, I ignored the wetness that was seeping through my jeans as I ran through a hundred different scenarios of my brother's whereabouts. Dead in a ditch after swerving off the road drunk or fighting the first person that looks at him down at the Wagon Wheel.

Cupping my face into my palms, I lowered my head and prayed for God to strengthen me in my time of need. To be with my brother, to welcome dad up to heaven and know I'll see him again one day. Tears began to fall as I concluded the prayer and took a deep breath. I ran off the porch and got into my truck, heading for the Wagon Wheel.

"What's wrong?" Trisha asked as I walked in the front doors.

Shaking my head, I asked as I leaned to one side of her to look into the bar, "Have you seen Chris?"

"No," she replied. "What's going on?"

"Is Elly here?"

"No, she's off today because of a baby shower for her friend, why? What's up?"

She must be at Jess's, I thought to myself as I turned to leave.

"Dylan!" Trisha shouted, startling me. "Please talk to me!"

Coming back over to her, I touched the side of her arm and said, "It's our Dad… He died and I think Chris is not in a good frame of mind."

"Oh," she replied. "I'm so sorry for your loss…"

"He's in a better place now, Trish," I said. "Thank you, though. But can you call my house if you find Chris? And call Jess or something?"

"Sure, what's your number?" She asked grabbing a pen and piece of paper.

"Don't you have it because of Chris?"

"Oh yeah, I keep forgetting this place doesn't have cell phones."

I smiled. "Yeah, so could you do that?"

"I will for sure," she replied.

"Thanks."

Leaving out the door of the Wagon Wheel, I got back into my truck and headed out to Roy's place to see if Elly knew where Chris could have possibly gone off to. If anyone could guess, she'd be the one.

Arriving to the farm, I noticed pink and blue balloons wrapped around the mailbox. An uneasy feeling set inside of me as I continued down the driveway and across the bridge. I felt bad interrupting the baby shower, but I had to find my brother.

Getting out of my truck, I jumped a little when Levi came out from the garage, startling me. "Hey Dylan... What's wrong?"

"Chris is gone and I don't know where. Our Dad died..."

"Oh man..." Levi said shaking his head. "I'm sorry to hear that, but sadly, Chris is not here."

"I was thinking Elly might know where he could have run off."

"She might know," Levi replied. "Let's go find out."

Levi accompanied me up to the farmhouse and went inside to fetch Elly from the festivities. Coming out to the patio, she asked with an agitated tone, "What is it, Dylan?"

"Do you know where Chris could have gone?"

"I don't date Chris anymore; I need to go back to the baby shower…" She paused and looked at Levi. "Thanks for dragging me out here."

As she opened the door, I said, "Frank died." She froze in place for a moment before turning around.

"I'm sorry to hear that…" Her words trailed off as her tone shifted to one of more understanding.

"If you can think of anywhere he might have gone… it'd be very helpful."

She looked up as she appeared to think about it. "I'd try Sparky's grave." She went inside and shut the door behind her. Sparky was the dog we had when we were a couple of teenagers.

"Okay, I'm going to go check that out."

"Take care man; give us a call when you find him," Levi said.

"I will," I replied. "Thanks for being such a good friend."

Heading back out to the truck, I dug my hands into my coat pocket as I hurried my steps through the darkness. As I opened my truck door, Ally was coming out of the gate that led into the field. "What are you doing out here?" I asked confused to why she wasn't in at the baby shower.

"Just getting some air…" she replied.

"Why aren't you with your friend and doing the baby shower thing?"

"I don't know… I stayed for a bit, but I had to just get out of there and go clear my head. Why are you here?"

"Chris went missing after he found out our Dad died."

"I'm so sorry about your Dad." Shaking her head, she continued, "This must be horrible; you don't have any idea where he could be?"

"No. I'm heading over to a spot Elly said she might have seen him."

"Could I go?" She asked.

I was surprised by the request. "Really?" I glanced back at the farmhouse, as I continued, "Wouldn't your kids miss you?"

She shook her head, "They are at Floyd and Margret's staying the night since this whole baby shower thing is going on."

"I see," I replied. I wanted her to go with me. The thought of having someone next to me when I found him sounded good. I wasn't sure what I was going to find out there. "Sure, if you want to come along that's fine. Want to go tell someone?"

She smiled. "Yeah, just hold on."

"Okay, I'll warm up the truck."

Getting into the cab of my truck I turned the key over and turned the heat up a little more so that she'd be comfortable. Watching as she ran up to the farmhouse, I smiled. I didn't know her much, but what I did know was that she wanted to come with me to find Chris, and I liked that.

We buried Sparky right next to a big boulder on the east side of the lake. The inn sat on the opposite side. It was about an hour and a half hike from the inn, or a twenty minute hike from a different access point to the lake.

On the drive over, Ally broke the silence and kind of caught me off guard. "Did you know that Sammy won't talk to strangers? You're the first male that he'd interact with outside of his father."

"Well I'm glad. He seems like a neat little kid."

She smiled as she looked out the window. "He really is… He's obsessed about that coin trick of yours. He won't stop talking about it. And now he makes Levi give him wheelbarrow rides when he goes out to get more wood." She laughed. "He seems happy out here; Olivia does too…"

"Good," I replied. "Living out in the country is probably a little different than city life."

She nodded. "It's nice not hearing sirens all the time. And the quietness you find out in the stillness of the evenings is priceless. The stars were so bright and numerous tonight on my walk."

I smiled as I replied, "The stars always remind me of God's beautiful design and purpose for our lives."

"I agree."

The silence returned between us in my truck, but this time I broke it. "So do the kids see their Dad? Or how's that work?" I asked.

She sighed heavily as it seemed a weight was dropped onto her shoulders. "I don't know. He says he wants them in the summer and then he changes his mind a few days later. He's flip-flopping all over the place and he keeps changing what he tells the kids. I was even like- Adam, just make up your mind and stick with it. They need consistency."

I nodded. "Sounds like a difficult time."

"It is," she agreed. "And the worst part about that guy is my parents are so in love with him that they keep trying to edge me back to him. They even kept a picture of him in their living room!"

I laughed a little. "Sounds like they should marry him."

She laughed. "I know, right?"

"You haven't thought about going back to him? For the kid's sake and all that?"

"No, I don't want that jerk back." I was hesitant to ask what happened, but I did start to ask, but stopped. She caught it and asked, "What were you going to say?"

"Nothing, never mind," I replied.

"No... you can't do that. You already started saying something. Just say it."

I glanced over at her and asked, "What happened

between you two?"

"Long version or short?" She asked.

"I'd like the short, if it'd work."

"He was a slimy guy."

"Okay," I laughed. "What's the long version?"

"Everything started out great. For instance, the first couple years of marriage we were in church all the time and then when the children came he was super into helping me and whatnot. Then he got this promotion at his job which began requiring more of his time. Which was totally fine, I'm not one of those women who nag their husband about working too much. And anyways, it started getting more and more that he 'had to work' or whatever. I'm talking, he went from being home by five, to six, seven and then it got to the point where he was leaving at six in the morning and getting home after one in the morning, and get this, sometimes he wasn't even coming home at all! What kind of life is that?"

"Wow."

"Yeah, but anyways, basically I found out he had a girlfriend and all these crazy issues with drugs. I couldn't handle it. That was no life I wanted and I had the Biblical reason for divorce, so I took it. And now I'm here. My kids seem happier and Jess knows a lot of good people, so I think it's for the best."

"I'm so sorry you went through all that," I said.

She looked at me and smiled, "It's okay. I'm sorry I went on and on… I shouldn't even be talking about myself right now. You just had your Dad die."

Waving my hand over to her, I shook my head. "No, I'm happy you are talking. It helps keep my mind off the fact my father is gone and my brother is missing...." Pausing for a moment, I realized I missed the cut-off for the access point. "Dang it," I said smacking the steering wheel. Pulling over to the side of the road I said, "We went too far. I was too focused on our conversation."

She laughed. "Snap, how far past did we go?"

Looking up and out of the windshield I just saw trees on both sides of the road. I had no idea. "No clue," I laughed.

She laughed. "I'm so sorry!"

I smiled over at her. "It's okay. We'll start heading back."

"Sounds good," she replied. "So what about you?"

"What about me?" I asked.

"Tell me about Dylan Holden."

"What do you want to know?"

She shrugged. "I just feel like I shared a lot and I don't know much about you. The balance is off right now, we need some weight on your side to even it out." She paused for a moment. "Wait, the table… you made that for Floyd. Tell me about your woodworking stuff."

"Well I make tables and chairs and whatnot."

"Well I know that, I own one."

"Really?" I asked surprised.

She blushed. "Yes, I bought one when I was at the Chattaroy Feed Store a while back, I didn't realize it was even yours until I brought it home and Jess pointed it out. She explained how you make furniture and sell it at the feed store."

"Well I'm flattered you picked one up," I replied with a grin.

"Don't let it go to your head, but I think you are pretty talented. You put a lot of detail that you just don't find in much furniture these days."

I nodded. "Thank you." I turned a little red in the face.

She laughed. "Don't be embarrassed! Embrace your inner awesomeness!"

I laughed.

Arriving at the access point just after nine, Ally and I got out of the truck and headed down the dirt path into the woods. The moonlight was bright enough to light our way, but I retrieved flashlights from the back just in case.

Coming to the water's edge, we began making our way up the shoreline towards the boulder where Sparky was buried.

"Do you think your brother's here with his truck not being parked back at the access point entrance?" She asked.

"I don't know..." I replied. "I have to try though."

As we arrived at the boulder, we found an empty bottle of whiskey that wasn't frozen over with ice. Bending at the knees as I picked it up, I turned to Ally. "We must have just missed him. He's been here." I looked across the lake and at the inn. "Maybe he is over at the inn?"

"What inn?" She asked.

"Silverback Inn, it was my Dad's and now it's our uncle Lenny's."

"I see. We can try there?"

"Yeah, I'm sure Lenny will let us crash out there for the night."

"Let's just head home," she replied.

"Okay," I replied. We began walking back towards the truck and Ally was near my side.

"I'm sorry," she said. "I just don't want to share a room with you, no offense."

"You'd have your own room, Ally," I laughed.

She took a breath of relief. "Oh thank goodness... I thought you wanted to share a room."

"Uh, no. I don't know you and I'm not that kind of dude."

"I'm not that kind of gal, so I felt super awkward." She sighed. "I'm glad, though, you aren't that kind of guy… you've never given me a reason to think that; I was just trying to be cautious."

Smiling, I asked, "So you want to crash out over there?"

"Sure, let's go." She seemed much more comfortable now that she realized I wasn't interested in that kind of thing with her.

We made it over to the inn by eleven and by no surprise Lenny was still awake. He had a horrible case of insomnia for all the time I've known him growing up. He'd spend hours staying up late watching TV.

When he opened the door he hugged me right away. "Dylan!" He said as he pulled back. "I hadn't heard from you or your brother all day, I've been biting my nails in anticipation."

"Chris is missing," I replied agitated. "Why would you leave a voicemail like that?"

"I'm sorry; I wasn't in my right mind. I didn't even call until the afternoon because of all the chaos that followed this morning." He looked over at Ally. "Who's this?" he asked with a raised brow.

"This is Ally; she's one of Jess's friends from Atlanta."

"I see," he said with a suspicious tone.

"It's not like that. Could we get two rooms for the night? We are tired of searching for Chris and need some shut eye."

"Absolutely. Let me grab my jacket and we'll go get you some keys over at the office."

Pillowing my head that evening, I closed my eyes and thought back to my childhood. One memory stuck out in my mind particularly. Chris, Dad and I were all on a row boat in the middle of the lake and we were fishing. It was one of my earliest childhood memories of all of us together having a good time. Dad was baiting our hooks when Chris suddenly began peeing off the back of the boat. Dad laughed and smiled as he shook his head and I joined him in the grin. That day we lost track of time out on the lake and we ended up fishing for nearly half the day. As I drifted off to sleep, I made a commitment to myself and God that I'd focus on those good and wholesome memories of my father instead of the bitterness and anger that he showed Chris and me.

FEBRUARY 11, 2011

The next day I woke up relatively early and just lay there, my thoughts spinning in my head about Chris. Where are you trying to go? I wondered as I watched the ceiling fan spin above my bed. A knock from my door broke into my thoughts. Glancing over at the alarm clock on the nightstand, I saw it was about six. I grabbed my coat that was draped over the chair at the table and headed for the door.

"You okay with us chatting a little?" Lenny asked, handing me a cup of coffee.

"Sure," I replied stepping out from the cabin and shutting the door behind me. We walked over to the office and had a seat inside on the couch in the lobby area.

"Your Father was a complicated man, Dylan," Lenny said before taking a drink of his coffee and setting it down on the coffee table.

"I would have to agree with that."

"Did you know about the room?" Lenny asked as his eyes fell over to the hallway that led back to some additional offices.

"Room?" I asked.

"Yeah, a hidden room in this building."

Shaking my head, I replied, "No." Dad had a secret room?

Lenny stood up and motioned for me to follow. Walking down the hallway I noticed all the pictures of the rewards and magazine articles along both sides of the walls. The Silverback used to be a big deal back in the eighties, but business trickled downward over the years, especially in the nineties when people began using the internet for marketing and making decisions on getaways. My dad's little newspaper ad suddenly wasn't relevant anymore and he was too stubborn to learn about internet marketing. He thought the internet was just a trend that would go away.

Coming into my dad's old office, Lenny pulled back the rug that was on the floor and revealed a square cut out of the floor with a handle. "Never knew about this…" I said softly.

"He was fairly private. I wouldn't take it to heart," Lenny said, looking up at me as he pulled up on the handle, moving the piece of floor up and out of the way.

Glancing down into the hole, it was dark until Lenny reached down and flipped on a light switch.

I immediately noticed my old bike from when I was a kid. I thought he had gotten rid of it years ago. Following Lenny down the ladder into the hole, I found myself in a room full of items from our childhood. "What is this place?"

"He kept all this stuff over the years. To remember the times he had spent with you and Chris."

"Why would he hide this from us? We thought he got rid of it all!"

Shrugging, Lenny replied, "He loved you boys more than you'll probably ever understand."

Spotting a safe over in the corner, I asked, "What's in there?"

"That's the cash he kept on hand. Quite a bundle if I do say so myself. He called this place his treasure room."

Walking along the shelves, I marveled at how many different things he kept from the days of old. Old report cards from our school years were framed, my old Pog collection, Chris's action figure that he loved to throw off the dock with a piece of fishing line attached to it. It was all here, in his treasure room. My eyes were soon watering as I was overwhelmed with the new-found love I had discovered our father had for us. Then I came across an envelope with my and Chris' name on it. Picking it up, I turned to Lenny.

"That's the letter he wrote you the day he found out he was going to die. He wanted you to have it after he passed on."

I began to open it when Lenny put his hand over mine. "Not here Dylan. You can read it, just not here."

"Why?"

"It's intense," Lenny replied.

"You know what it says?"

"I can guess at what it says."

Nodding, I slipped the envelope into my pocket. Continuing to inspect the room, my thoughts drifted back to Chris. "You have any idea where Chris could be?"

"Let's go back up to the lobby," Lenny said.

Following after him, we went back up out of the room and into the lobby. We took a seat back down on the couch in front of our cups of coffee. Lenny took another sip and said, "I don't know where Chris ran off to, I haven't seen him since I've been here."

The office door opened, and the bell chimed. Glancing over, I smiled as I saw it was Ally. "Hey…" she said softly. "Am I interrupting? I can go."

"No," I replied. "It's okay."

Shaking her head, she said, "I can tell I'm interrupting. I'm just going to go for a walk along the lake."

I watched over my shoulder through the window as she headed down to the lake. The sun hadn't fully risen, but there was enough light out to create a dim blue hue outside.

"You like her," Lenny said.

Shaking my head, I said, "Nah." Lenny didn't need to know about my personal life or my feelings about Ally. I was still trying to figure them out for myself.

"No, I can tell these things, Dylan," Lenny said shaking my shoulder. "It's okay if you like a gal; you aren't getting any younger."

"She's fresh out of a divorce. She was married for, like, six years and has kids."

"You said she was from Portland?" He asked.

"No, Atlanta."

"Oh. What'd she do there?" Lenny asked.

"I don't know." Recalling the nursery she did for Jess and Levi, I remembered that she was an interior designer. "Oh wait, she was an interior designer."

"Oh wow, in Atlanta? That's impressive in a big city."

Nodding, I replied, "Yeah. So, no ideas on Chris?"

"Nope. If I were you, though, I would just double back over your tracks and try friends, work, places he frequents."

"Okay," I sighed heavily.

Lenny patted my back. "You'll find him. He's a little unpredictable and scatter-brained, but he's not stupid. I'm sure he's okay in the sense he's alive."

"He is kind of stupid, Lenny... he was home drinking yesterday and then got in his car and drove."

"He's just hurting."

I agreed with a nod and stood up. Shaking Lenny's hand, I said, "Thanks for everything; I'm glad my Dad could trust you with the inn. After I get this Chris issue sorted out, I'll drop off the tables and we can move forward with the next phase."

"Sounds good, no rush. Take care."

Walking out the office door, I pulled out the letter. I began reading the letter as I headed down to the boat dock to sit out on the end of the dock. Lenny came out of the office and got in his truck, taking off somewhere.

Dylan,

Today I found out that I have only a few months to live, could be less. On the car ride back out to the Silverback after I found out the news, I spent a great deal of time reflecting over my life and the choices I made in raising you and Chris. First off, I know the visits over to your house to kick your butts into shape probably ended up doing more harm than good in the long run. I sit here now, in my little room in the back of the Silverback, on my bed alone with my thoughts. I am so sorry for the way I had treated you and your brother. I always thought I was doing the right thing until today. When I realized I hadn't seen nor heard from either of you in a while.

I'm writing this letter, not to apologize only, but to tell you about your mother, Elyse. You see, she never died; she's actually alive and well with a different family in Lincoln City, Oregon. I have tears in my eyes as I write this because it's been a secret I've kept from you boys since she left us so long ago. I never had the heart to tell you she moved on. I always wished she'd someday return and make amends with the both of you. But I fear if I don't write this down, you might never know the truth.

Take care of each other.

I love you both,

Dad

Raising my watering eyes up, I looked across the lake as the sunrise came up. The beauty of the morning was eclipsed by the feeling of betrayal I felt not only by my own mother, but by my father. How could he never tell us about our mom? I felt angry, sad and hurt all at once as I glared into the still and quiet waters that lay before me. You sure have impeccable timing, Father! I thought to myself.

Suddenly a hand touched my shoulder. Looking up, I saw it was Ally and quickly wiped my eyes. "Why do you keep catching me in these awkward moments," I replied harshly.

"Sorry," she replied curtly as she turned to leave the dock.

"Wait, Ally," I said, jumping up to my feet to catch up to her. "I'm sorry…"

"It's fine Dylan. Are we about ready to go?"

"Yeah," I replied with a nod. "The Wagon Wheel opens soon for breakfast; we'll get some food and ask about Chris."

On our way over to the Wagon Wheel, I pulled into a gas station to fuel up. Leaving her in the truck, I went inside and paid. It was Jack working the counter that morning and when he saw Ally out the window in the truck, he gave me a smile and nod. Jack was a buddy of mine who I played football with back in High School.

"Jack, it's not like that, she's just a friend."

"At eight o'clock in the morning?" He replied with a laugh. "Whatever you say, man."

Shaking my head, I smiled and paid for my gas before heading back out to the truck. As I put my wallet in the glove box in front of Ally, she asked, "What were you two talking about?"

"He's an old friend and was thinking we were together," I replied.

"Why are people like that?" She asked with a slight agitation in her tone. "Two people of the opposite sex can't just hang out?" She laughed.

"It's ridiculous for someone to think we were together?" I asked.

"No," she replied with a laugh. "That's not a ridiculous idea…" she turned red. "I mean."

"I get what you are saying. I agree, I think it was more of the eight AM sleepover implication he was getting at," I replied smiling over at her.

Getting over to the Wagon Wheel that morning, the parking lot only had a couple cars in it.

After we were seated and waiting on our meals to arrive at the table, a familiar face popped out from the kitchen. It was Missy; she looked rather chipper and busy as she rushed around the restaurant doing various tasks. I kept my eyes locked on her as I wondered if she had found out about my dad already. There was no way she had heard the news.

"Who's that?" Ally asked, joining my gaze at Missy.

"Missy, she's the owner here. She had a thing with my Dad… I don't think she knows."

"She's far too happy to know. Look at that smile," Ally replied sadly.

Seeing her come our direction, I mulled around the idea of telling her. I'd hate for her to read it in the paper after I left here. I had to tell her.

"Hey, Dylan, nice seeing you here so early," Missy said. "Who's your lady friend?"

"Ally, she's Jess's cousin."

Ally extended a hand and shook Missy's. "Nice meeting you, Missy?"

"Yes, my name is Marissa, but everyone calls me Missy." As they released from their handshake, Missy continued, "I heard that guy got out of ICU."

"Yep. I'm glad that whole thing turned out okay." I paused for a moment before I blurted out, "We need to talk."

Missy looked at me, "Oh?"

My words weighed heavily as I said, "Yes…"

Looking into my eyes, she knew instantly. "I can't, I'm busy," she said as she began to walk away.

Leaping up from the booth, I chased after her and stopped her. I turned her around, and she began crying into my shoulder as I embraced her with a hug. "He can't be gone…"

"I'm sorry," I replied.

As she slowed her crying, she wiped her eyes. "He was just in here a few days ago."

"Yeah?" I pleaded with my eyes for her to continue.

She nodded. "He was sitting up at the bar drinking a water with lemon, telling me about how sad he was about you and Chris. He had hope still though, like he always did for both of you."

My eyes watered, but I held back my tears. My father's disappointment in me stung. He was gone, and I never had a chance to make him proud.

"I'm sorry. I just can't believe he's never going to come walking through those doors to come see me again."

I nodded, but remained silent.

"How's Chris handling it?" She asked.

Shaking my head, I replied, "He's missing. He found out before I did and then he up and vanished."

"He was here last night. I saw him on the surveillance tapes when I reviewed them this morning."

My heart began to race. Another fight? Is he in jail? "Did he fight?" I asked.

"No. He just sat at the end of the bar, on the last stool, drinking a whiskey on the rocks…" She paused. "I should have known something wasn't right. He's usually screaming at the TV when he's not fist-fighting someone."

"Missy, we have a delivery you need to sign for in the back," a guy from the kitchen said, interrupting our conversation.

"I best get going, Dylan. Enjoy your meals. It's on the house today. Let me know if I can do anything for you boys."

"Thanks," I replied.

Returning back to the booth, I sat down with Ally. I took a deep breath in and let the air escape my lips. I was glad he didn't fight anyone last night, but knowing he was most likely depressed over our father's passing tore me up inside.

"You okay?" Ally asked.

Nodding, I replied as I watched Missy go into the kitchen, "It's just hard to see other's pain, like Missy. I can keep my own self together pretty decently… but to see someone else hurt, kills me. Does that make sense?"

She nodded. "It does. God's here for you in your time of need. Don't ever forget that."

I smiled. "I couldn't imagine getting through this

without God."

After finishing our breakfast, Ally and I headed back over to my house to see if Chris had come home last night after his visit to the Wagon Wheel. Sure enough, upon arriving, Chris's car was parked out in the driveway. If I would have just gone home last night, I would have found him, I thought to myself as I shook my head. I was relieved he was safe, but a little irritated with him as I pulled in next to his car.

As I began getting out of the truck, Ally said, "I'll hang back."

"Okay, you can get out and go check out my shop or whatever, if you want."

"I'll do that. I'm kind of curious where the magic happens."

I grinned. "It's nothing fancy. It's right around the corner of the house in the back."

"Okay," she smiled, getting out of the truck. "Good luck with Chris."

Walking up the front steps of the house, I took a deep breath in as I turned the handle of the doorknob. Coming into the living room, I saw him passed out on the couch with his baseball glove on his chest. Seeing him lying there sleeping, I couldn't help but be overcome with emotion. He was safe, and the glove made me realize how hurt he was by the loss of our father. He really did care about Dad, even though he was upset and angry with him.

Walking up to the couch, I bent a knee down and said, "Brother."

He blinked his eyes open and smiled. His smile only lasted for a moment as if he had no memory of yesterday, and then he must have recalled because his smile fell away and was replaced with a frown.

"I never got a chance to make things right with Dad… I thought I had more time," Chris said, wiping a runaway tear from his watery eyes.

Shaking my head, I replied, "Me too."

"He's just… gone? I don't know how to deal with this, Dylan… I really thought he was lying, I never believed he could die…" Chris said, letting his words trail off. His voice was strained, and lacked hope and strength.

"You got to give it to God," I responded.

Shaking his head, he sat up on the couch and I sat next to him. "God? You know I don't…"

"I know, but He's the only one that can make you feel better. You're never going to find the peace you are seeking in the bottom of a bottle."

"I know," he replied softly. "What's weird is I don't feel like I want to fight anymore. It's almost like all my energy and passion for righting the wrong in the world evaporated." He relaxed back into the couch. "I work in an hour… and I don't even care about that."

"You don't want to lose your job, Chris," I replied. "You need that job."

"Why? What's the point?" he asked.

Putting my hand on his shoulder, I said, "You already know of your responsibilities, I don't need to list them for you." I paused for a moment. "You're pretty broken up about this for someone who wouldn't even visit Dad."

He replied, "That's what hurts the most. I never went and saw him... I was just so angry. Now I'm just left with this empty feeling inside, like something is missing."

"I know you were angry with him, but you know he was smart."

"Yeah, so?" he replied.

"He found God at the end of his life, Chris."

"Yeah, but he just reverted back to his old ways. You saw him in the hospital. He was a jerk, just like before... he didn't ever change."

Shaking my head, I replied, "Becoming a born-again Christian doesn't make you become this perfect and supreme being. It washes the sins away from your life, endows peace, grants you an eternity with God and gives you the Holy Spirit who will help guide your life..."

"I just want this emptiness to go away."

"Chris that empty feeling inside..."

"Yeah?"

"That's your need of God. Maybe you didn't notice it until now, but that's a need for God we all have. You see, everyone has a God-sized hole in their life and they are trying to fill it. Sometimes that's with a bottle, sometimes it's with a big house and fancy cars. Maybe even a relationship, like with a parent. Whatever it is, the satisfaction we all desire in this life doesn't come from the possessions we have or anything that we can actually do on our own on this earth. It comes from God."

"I don't need preached at. If you could just get it through your thick skull that it was me who had the Christian friend when we were kids, you'd realize I never bought into the whole God thing. The only reason why you even became a Christian was because of Andrew, so stop it with God!" Chris replied standing up quickly.

Andrew was Chris's friend who went to church every Sunday morning, Sunday night and even on Wednesdays. He was the reason I ever found Christ. It was through a summer camp that I accepted Jesus as my Savior. Andrew invited Chris and myself along one summer when we were ten years old and ever since then, I've been a dedicated follower of Jesus.

"We're out of milk. I'm going to get a gallon at the corner store and I'll be back in a minute, but I gotta head out to work soon." Chris kept his eyes down as he stepped out the front door and left. His pain was written all over his face. He was searching for a comfort that wasn't going to come from any source outside of God. The hardest part was knowing the truths and peace of God, while I watched my brother struggle against it. He might have lost his desire to fight, but there was a spiritual battle raging inside of him. I could see it in his eyes and feel it with his words; I only could hope the outcome would result in God winning.

I stood up and peered out the window as Chris pulled out of the driveway. I was worried about him more than ever, so I lowered my head and said a prayer for him.

Ally came walking in the front door as I concluded my prayer. She asked, "How'd that go?"

"It went as expected. I tried sharing God a little with him and he almost seemed interested, but got uncomfortable and peaced out."

Ally nodded. "It's sad how this world needs God so badly, but they just refuse to acknowledge Him. I hope he comes around, Dylan, I really do. I don't mean to change the subject on you so quickly, but my curiosity is getting the better of me. Can you answer me a question about one of the tools I found?"

"Sure," I replied with a smile. Ally's request was a pleasant distraction. We ventured outside and to the shop. Coming inside, she led me over to my workbench and picked up my story stick.

"This thing," she said turning around with it dangling between her fingers. "It looks like a ruler, but it's not... and there are little pieces of metal sticking out of it."

Nodding, I replied, "That's a story stick. You know how table legs all match?"

"Yeah, what about it?" She asked.

"Come see," I said, taking the story stick, we went over to the tables I had been working on for the Silverback and I pushed the stick up against a leg. "They all match because of this story stick. I make it after I craft the first leg."

"Interesting," she said, smiling as she bent down next to me to look at the table leg. Her closeness was comfortable, and I could smell the perfume she had on. Rubbing her thumb against the table leg, she let her thumb drag across the grooves slowly. "It's so perfect."

Nodding, "It's by design. Kind of like how the world started out."

She smiled and rose to her feet. I stood up with her and she glanced over all the tables in my shop. "You sure have a lot of tables."

"Yeah, I'm obsessed with tables."

"Why?" she asked with a serious tone.

I laughed. "I'm just kidding. It's a project I'm working on at the inn. We're doing some renovations and my uncle needed a bunch of tables."

She smiled, "That's neat, your helping, I took the liberty of looking around a little while I was there, it's beautiful."

I nodded. "I wanted to make my Dad proud of me… and since I lost my chance with taking over the inn, I think helping with the renovations could do that…" My words trailed off.

"You can still make him proud with what you're doing to help your uncle."

I smiled. "Yeah."

Her eyes fell on the clock over on the wall. "My kids are probably anxious for me to pick them up. Could you drop me off over at Floyd's? I'm sure Margret or Floyd can give me a ride back to Jess's."

"Sure," I replied.

As we pulled up the driveway of Floyd's and I parked in front of the house in the roundabout, she turned to me.

"I know I am probably beating a dead horse at this point but I am sorry about your Dad, and uh, Thanks for bringing me along to find Chris; it was an adventure."

Nodding, I replied, "It was nice having you come along, Ally."

Getting out of the truck, she turned and said, "This might be a little forward, but do you want to do Valentine's Day dinner together? Maybe?"

I had completely forgotten that the holiday was even approaching, but I knew I couldn't refuse the offer. "Sure," I replied smiling. "I'll pick you up at about three. That way we can go see a movie before dinner."

Smiling back at me, she nodded. "Sounds perfect." She left the side of my truck and skipped a little on her way up to the door. As I put my truck back into drive, I couldn't help but grin the entire ride back to my house. She was a cute gal and she seemed serious about God, which I liked. I just knew she had a lot of baggage and didn't know how the Lord wanted this to go. I prayed on the car ride home for discernment, and for the Lord to press on my heart His will in regards to Ally.

Chris was already home from getting milk when I arrived back at the house. As I walked inside, I saw him sitting at the kitchen table eating a bowl of cereal. "Why aren't you at work?"

"Personal day," he replied curtly.

"Okay." Taking a seat the table, I continued, "I don't know how to say this… So, I'll just show you." Retrieving the letter from my back pocket, I unfolded it and pushed it across the table to him.

He read it as he continued to eat his cereal. He didn't say anything, but instead just continued eating.

"What are you thinking?" I asked.

He put a finger up and then pointed at his bowl. He didn't seem to have a desire to speak while he ate. The minutes felt like hours as he took his time eating. Then, he finally finished. He stood up, put his bowl in the sink and then proceeded upstairs and into his room.

Going after him, I pushed open his bedroom door to find him packing a duffle bag with clothes. "What are you doing?"

"I'm going to see Mom."

"You can't."

"I can, and I am."

Shaking my head, I got in front of him on his way back to his closet. "Brother, you can't just get in your car and go see her. You'll lose your job."

"I don't care about that." He side-stepped around me and continued to the closet.

I pleaded with him. "C'mon, you can't just jet out of here. I can't go with you if you leave now."

"I didn't ask you to go with me," he replied.

"Why are you doing this? We don't even know where she lives or anything about her other than her first name and the city."

"Pretty sure everyone knows everyone in that town. It's fairly small."

"Sure, it might be small, but it's going to take some time."

Chris stopped and shouted at me, "Leave me alone, dude! I'm leaving!"

Putting my hands up, I backed away. "Whatever, Bro… I thought we could just go together, find our mom together." Leaving his room, I shut the door quietly as I went back downstairs.

He's out of control. There's no way he's going to make it to Lincoln City without crashing his car. I will not bail him out of jail or come rescue him this time. Last time was bad enough, I almost went to jail for years over saving him; I'm not jeopardizing my future again or wasting another minute on him.

Picking up the phone in the kitchen, I cleared Chris out of my mind. I needed to get those tables over to the inn and borrow Levi's trailer to do it. Then, I could start on the next phase of furniture for the inn.

"Hello?" Roy answered the phone.

"How's it going, Roy?" I asked politely.

"It's going okay… Sorry to hear about your father passing."

"Thank you," I replied.

"It warms my heart, as I'm sure it does yours, knowing that he secured his spot in Heaven."

I sighed with a relief. "I'm quite happy about that fact."

"We miss you out at the church Dylan; you should really start attending more."

"I know, I've just been so swamped, it's hard."

"I know how that can be. We have to allow God priority over our life though. But anyways, did you need to speak with Levi?"

"Yes for a minute if he's not too busy."

"Just a moment," Roy replied, setting the phone down.

"Hello?" Levi said.

"Hey, I found Chris."

"Oh good."

"Yeah… I need a favor."

"Name it."

"That trailer, I need to borrow it to move some tables out to the Silverback."

"Alright," he replied and then paused. "How about in an hour? I'll come over then."

"Okay." Chris came down the stairs with a duffle bag in hand as he headed for the front door. "I'll see you then," I said to Levi, hanging up the phone. I ran after Chris out the front door.

Loading his bag into the back seat of his car, Chris began to get in. I darted down the porch steps and out to the road and in front of his car so he couldn't pull forward from the curb. "Chris…"

Rolling down his window, Chris yelled, "Get out of the way, Dylan, I'm going to find Mom, and you aren't going to stop me."

"Just wait for me to go with you, Bro."

"When? You got this and that going on all the time, I don't want to wait."

"We can go in a few days, we need to have Dad's funeral. There's a better way to do this."

Shutting off his car, he said, "Two days?"

"A few," I replied. "We need to go to Dad's funeral… usually they have those pretty quick, so right after that."

"Fine, okay," Chris replied softly.

Coming over to his driver side window, I leaned down to speak with him and put my hand on his shoulder. "Mom's been there for a while; we'll find her. This way works better anyways; you can call Ken and let him know what's going on so you don't lose that job."

Looking up at me, Chris shook his head and turned the key back over. My nerves unhinged as he revved the car up. "You know what? I'm not waiting, I'm going now. You thought you could run the inn without me, so I'll leave without you."

"Don't, Chris," I pleaded.

Shaking his head, he looked at me in the eyes and said, "I have to find her." He put the car into drive and peeled out. As he took off down the street, I watched his tail lights fade into the distance, worry came over me. My brother was on a dark and lonely path.

FEBRUARY 14, 2011

The funeral for my father was yesterday. It was a small group of people. Missy was there, and even Ally, Jess, Levi and Elly came to pay respects and support me. For family though, it was just Lenny and myself, since the rest of the family had passed on. My father was the youngest of three siblings. Knowing dad was in a better place, I choose to put the funeral behind me, and began getting ready for Ally's and my date that was tonight.

Up in my room, I gave myself a squirt of cologne and changed into a nice white polo for the evening. Hopefully Ally didn't get too dolled up for our date tonight, I wouldn't want to feel underdressed, I thought to myself as I grabbed the keys off the kitchen counter. Grabbing my coat, I was out the door and off to pick her up.

With a white skirt and a jean jacket on, Ally looked cute but a little cold as she waited out on the patio bench in front of Roy's house. I couldn't help but smile as I walked up the sidewalk towards the house. She looked amazing. Rising to her feet, she grinned at me as I approached.

"You ready?" I asked.

"Yes," she replied with a slight bow of a knee.

Sammy was peeking through the window that sat above the bench. He was smiling ear-to-ear as he looked at me. "Looks like we have a watcher," I said with a laugh.

Glancing over her shoulder, she saw Sammy and smiled. "He's quite excited that I'm going to a movie and dinner with you."

"Oh yeah? How's Olivia feel about it?"

She looked back at me, "She's not so glad. She kept asking me what Dad would think about it."

"Yeah, she's a little bit older…"

"Yep, she struggles with the idea of a new life here, even though she enjoys it."

"I'm sure. The movie we're going to see starts at four. We should get going that direction."

"Let's go!" she replied.

As I held out my arm, Ally grabbed onto it and I led her out to the truck. Helping her into the passenger seat, I couldn't stop smiling, which was strange, since I had just buried my dad; but just being around Ally made me not worry about all the bad going on.

Getting into the theater and taking our seats, we had two sodas, a large popcorn and a box of chocolate caramels. Glancing over at Ally midway through the movie, I couldn't help but notice how gorgeous she looked in the low lighting of the movie theater. Her skin glowed from the light of the screen and her smile was perfect as always. There wasn't a different place in the world I wanted to be in that moment.

Midway through the movie, I suddenly felt her hand grasped onto mine that was on the armrest that separated us. Waves of warmth rushed over me at her touch. Shortly after that, I put my arm around her shoulder and scooted closer to her. She fit perfect in my arm. I could tell neither of us wanted to leave the theater, we even sat through the credits, just letting ourselves pretend like we cared about the costume designers and all the people involved in making the movie. But really, I think we both were so into the moment and each other we didn't want it to ever end.

On the way to the restaurant, Ally's cell phone rang causing me to jump in my seat. She laughed. "You don't hear that very often, do ya?" I shook my head over at her and she glanced down at her phone. "It's Jess. I'd better answer it," she said.

"Hello?"

She listened.

"What do you mean you can't find Olivia?" Ally replied with a worried tone.

I nodded over to her as I pulled over and headed back

towards Chattaroy. She didn't have to say anything; I knew we needed to go back to the farm.

"We're on our way," she said before hanging up the phone. Turning to me, she said, "I'm so sorry. Olivia up and vanished after dinner and they can't find her."

"No need to apologize," I replied. "Don't worry about it."

"I really enjoyed the movie, Dylan…" I knew what she really meant.

"It was nice," I replied. "Do you know where Olivia might have gone off to?"

Ally looked out the window and was quiet for a moment. "She really likes the creek… maybe she's down there? I don't really know… ugh."

"We'll find her, don't worry."

"You can just drop me off, Dylan, you don't need to stay and help find my little defiant child."

"No, I want to help. More people looking will help us find her faster." Smiling at her and trying to reassure her, I grabbed her hand.

She smiled at me as she wrapped her fingers into mine that was on the seat between us. "Thank you."

Arriving back at Roy's, we parked in front of the garage and grabbed the flashlights I had stashed behind the seat. Walking down the hillside along the creek, we split up to find Olivia.

Coming to the bridge's underside, an old favorite

hiding spot of mine, I pointed my flashlight into the water and then up against the wall that sat under the bridge. There she was. "Olivia," I said, coming up to her. She was sitting with her knees up to her chest and an angry look on her face. "What's wrong?"

"You!" she snapped at me as she turned slightly to look away.

I took a deep breath, walked up to her and sat down next to her. Pulling my knees up to my chest to match hers, I set my flashlight down and said, "Me?"

"Yeah! Ever since Mommy started talking to you, she talks about Daddy less and less... I miss my Daddy!"

I nodded. "I miss my Daddy too."

Her angry face softened. "Where's your Daddy?"

"Heaven," I replied delicately.

"He died?" Her eyes widened.

"Yeah, not too long ago, in fact."

"I'm sorry for your loss," she replied.

I laughed a little inside, knowing she probably didn't understand what she was saying. "Thank you, Olivia."

"You should leave my Mommy alone. She doesn't need you. She has Sammy and me, and she even has Daddy."

"I just like hanging out with your Mom. I'm not going to take her from you, ever." She seemed okay with what I said, so I continued, "We're just friends and like hanging out. That's what adults do sometimes."

Ally came up to the bridge and breathed a heavy sigh of relief. "Olivia!" she shouted. "You scared everyone half to death! Get your butt up to the farmhouse and into your room, right now! I will be there in a minute to talk about your actions tonight."

Olivia glanced at me, and stood up and stomped off up the hill and out of sight towards the house. Turning back to me, Ally cleared her voice and smiled, "Thanks, Dylan. I really appreciate you helping find her."

"No problem," I replied.

"Hey, speaking of going missing, have you heard from Chris? I meant to ask earlier, but spaced it," she said as I stood up from under the bridge.

"He called for a second when he got into town to just let me know he made it safely. He's staying at the Seagull Inn while he hunts for our mom."

"You should go there."

"He left without me; it'd be stupid to go with a second car."

"Just fly there," she insisted.

"Why are you pushing me to go?" I asked curiously.

"It's your brother all by himself looking for your mom. You want to be there, don't you?"

"Yeah, but-"

Ally took a step closer to me and touched my arm. "You'll always have a reason not to do something you're scared of… but sometimes the scariest thing in the world is exactly what we need to do."

"What if she doesn't have a reason for leaving us?" I asked with a nervous tone in my voice. "That's what worries me the most."

Shaking her head, she replied, "You have to have faith, Dylan... And I know you do. If there is one thing I know about you, it's that your faith carries you along. I've admired how you have handled your Father's passing with such strength." She let her fingers slide down the sides of my arms along my muscles as she continued, "You are courageous and an inspiration. Don't let your faith waver in the presence of fear."

Nodding, I replied, "Okay, I will go."

FEBRUARY 15, 2011

Coming out of the airport terminal at Lincoln City, I was surprised by the strong smell of the ocean that was evident in the air as I stepped outside. Getting into the back of a cab, I asked the driver to take me to the Seagull Inn where I knew my brother Chris was staying.

As we drove through the little town of Lincoln City, I couldn't help but think about my mother and how she visited many of the shops there. Seeing a grocery store, I thought about her and envisioned her pulling up in a car to go get groceries. It was so strange since just a week ago I thought she was dead. But now she is not dead; it turned out she had another life. Why'd she leave us? I kept asking myself on the ride over to the hotel. What would she think about when she saw us?

After paying my cab fair, I noticed Chris' car in the parking lot at the hotel. It was parked along the farthest edge of the lot and the ocean waves were crashing up on the shore off in the distance behind. He really did it, he drove all the way here, I thought, smiling. Thankfully he made it in one piece. Walking into the hotel lobby, I asked for Chris' room. They refused to give me the room number and instead called him, thus ruining my surprise.

"He's in room six-one-six," the hotel clerk said.

"Thanks," I replied. Grabbing my duffle bag from the floor, I headed out the door and over across the parking lot to his room.

Chris was standing in the doorway smiling. "You came!" He shouted over the cool breeze that was blowing.

"Sure did," I replied as I walked into the room.

Tossing my duffle bag in the corner, I asked, "So, any leads on Mom?"

"It's tough, man. I just have an old photograph I pulled from that photo album years ago. I've been asking local stores if they knew the woman."

"That's going to take forever. Let's see if we can get a last name, the note did say she had a different family here, have you called and asked Lenny if he knows what her last name might be?" I asked.

"No."

I walked over to the phone and dialed out to the Silverback back in Chattaroy to see if Lenny might know about our mom's last name.

"Silverback Inn, this is Lenny."

"Hey, it's me, Dylan. I'm in Lincoln City with Chris."

"Oh wow, you decided to go?"

"Yeah, what could you tell us about our mom, Elyse? Do you know by chance what last name she could be under?"

"She was married to your father but she never took his last name, so I doubt she'd be under that... hm. Even if she did, she left and wouldn't have kept it. You know what you could try? Her maiden name, Miles."

"Okay, we'll go with that."

"Sounds good, I'll see if I can dig anything up in your Dad's stuff down in that room. By the way, I deposited a check from your Dad's estate into your bank this morning, so that should help with your two's venture. It included this quarter's dividends."

"Thanks Lenny," I said as I hung up the phone.

"Mom's maiden name is Miles; she never took Dad's to begin with." I began wondering maybe she was never into the marriage to dad? She did after all never take his last name. There was no telling for sure on anything. There were no memories for us of our mother, outside of the ones our father told us. But who really knows if any of that was even true.

We went with using the phone book first and we found a listing under an 'E. Miles' that lived off a road named Island Drive, just south of town along the ocean side.

"This could be her!" I said excitedly. Picking up the phone, I dialed the number. It dead rang forever without a voicemail. Hanging it back up, I sighed and said, "No answer."

Chris smiled as he patted my back. "Let's go see her; we have the address."

I nodded and we ran out of the hotel room to go get in the car. I felt a little apprehensive with Chris as he got into the driver seat. "Hey man, I can drive…" I said, trying to be delicate as possible about the situation.

"If it's about drinking, you don't have to worry about it, Bro," he said as he got into the driver seat.

"You quit?" I asked with raised eyebrows.

Nodding, he said, "Ever since I got here and could smell the ocean… I just felt so much better, almost like I found a part of myself here. Maybe that's why Mom loves it here. Something about the air."

"Whatever works," I replied smiling as we got into the car. I was relieved to hear him say he wasn't drinking. Could a little ocean smell really curb an addiction? I wasn't sure, but I wasn't going to question him about it.

Pulling up the driveway of the address we had, the whole property sat on a slight incline which pointed towards the ocean. The constant sound of crashing waves in the distance was soothing the insecurity I had buried within my soul. I worried about meeting my mother for the first time. The lawn on the property was neatly trimmed and had a white picket fence that ran along the outskirts of the yard. Stones fitted together and made an elegant walkway up to the house. My nerves were on edge with every step on the way up to the door. This looked like a typical house of the American dream. Is this where she's been this whole time?

"Hello?" A woman answered the door. She looked thin, tall and blonde. She looked older, but not too old. Thinking of the old photographs that we had seen of our mother, she didn't look much like her.

"Hi, we are looking for an Elyse Miles?" I asked.

Shaking her head, she replied, "There is nobody here by that name." She began closing the door, and I put my hand up on the door.

"Wait, do you know anyone by that name in this town?"

She looked to think for a moment. "No, I am afraid I don't know anyone even by the name of Elyse. My name is Eleanor Miles."

"Sorry for bothering you, Thank you for your time," Chris said softly as he turned back towards the driveway.

We walked back to the car. On the way to the curb, I glanced out at the ocean and said, "We might never find her, Bro…"

"We'll find her," Chris said confidently.

"And then what?" I asked as we got back into the car.

"Then we can ask her why she left, what happened… find out the truth Dad hid from us. We could have a mom again, Dylan."

"Maybe," I replied. "Let's not get ahead of ourselves.

We need to be realistic. She left us. I don't know why, but she is a mother who left her children and didn't appear to look back. Isn't it strange she never took Dad's last name?"

Chris shrugged. "I don't know. I don't know anything anymore."

We were both in the mood for some seafood that night, so we headed down to Phill's Crab Shack on the pier. The restaurant walls were filled with fishing poles, anchors and other various ocean-related decorations. It was a loud and busy atmosphere, but the food was delicious.

"How's everything back home?" Chris asked, voice slightly elevated as he tried to talk over the other conversations in the restaurant.

"With what?"

"I don't know… it just sounded like the right thing to ask. How was Dad's funeral?"

"It was small… but it was nice. Levi and everyone showed up."

"Elly?" Chris asked.

I nodded.

"That's good they were all there for you…" He took a sip of his soda.

"Oh, here's something new. I went on a date with Ally."

Chris grinned. "I saw that coming. How'd it go?"

"It was fun. It was just last night, actually."

"Wow," he replied. Wiping his mouth with his napkin, Chris leaned in and asked, "Why'd you come here, Dylan?"

"I told you I wanted to come, just not immediately. You know you probably lost your job?"

"Oh well, Tyler will take my spot, I'm sure. Besides that's not what I want to do with the rest of my life anyways. I needed a good excuse to get out of that job."

"Yeah, I'm sure. But you don't have a job to go back to now."

"I'm sure I'll figure something out… Or maybe I'll stay here after I find Mom. She might want to get to know me."

"You're thinking way too optimistically about this whole thing," I warned.

"I don't think so, Dylan. She's our Mom and we are her kids."

"We'll see," I replied.

After dinner, we headed outside to walk the pier. We were bundled up in our coats to keep the bite of the cool breeze at bay, but the coldness didn't stop us from enjoying the beautiful sunset that was setting across the ocean. The red, pink and yellow hues in the sky were awesome and I thanked God for His beautiful design in that moment. We stopped at the pier's railing.

"I miss Elly," Chris said out of nowhere. Shaking his head, he continued, "I think my drinking got way too out of control."

I nodded in agreement. "We make mistakes. Maybe she'll take you back."

"I don't know… I messed up pretty big."

"Just ask for her forgiveness. That's all you can do."

"Yeah," he replied. He looked over at me and said, "On the drive out here, I had a lot of time to think."

"I bet you did--you never got that radio fixed."

He laughed. "Yeah, I'm glad I had the time to think though, Dylan. I thought about what you said about God and how we all have this big hole in our life."

"Oh yeah?" I replied, my interest was piqued. Could Chris be finally coming around to God?

"If we all have this big God-sized whole, and you have God… your hole is filled."

"Yes…"

"But what's it filled with? I don't see you go to church very often anymore, sure you don't drink or have sex, but you aren't in your Bible or anything… I just don't see how you are different than anyone else."

I felt convicted by my brother's words, even though that was not his intention. God was speaking to me in that moment. I replied to Chris, "I have inner peace… I'm slacking quite a bit in my walk right now with the Lord, but that doesn't change who God is. It's His peace, love and comfort that keeps me. My faith is always here."

"Slacking?" He sighed as he directed his eyes back to the ocean view. "You mean you haven't been following the rules." He laughed a little under his breath. "I don't get why Christians have to follow all these stupid rules."

"The rules don't give you the peace, the Holy Spirit of God does. The rules and recommendations for how to live your life is God letting you in on how to get through this thing called life. It's like an instruction manual. Sure, you can live life without the instructions. But life's a lot easier if you have the instructions to go along with it; otherwise you are just swinging in the dark and missing out on blessings."

"I see," he replied with a nod. "Thanks for more to think about. But I think if we can find Mom, I'll feel a lot better."

"We'll see," I replied. I could tell he was trying to steer back away from the God talk.

Back to the hotel that evening, I fetched my Bible from my duffle bag and dove into God's word. I felt kind of silly reading after feeling convicted, but I know that was just the devil trying to toy with my mind. He wanted me to feel stupid. As I prayed over my Bible reading, I prayed for my brother and for Lenny back at the inn. Even for Olivia and Sammy and Ally. By the time I finished praying, I felt relieved and my conscious felt a little lighter. Why'd I ever slack on this stuff? It's so good for the soul.

Sitting down at the table in the hotel room, I pulled the corded phone over to me and called Roy's house to speak with Ally. Turning away from Chris, who was on the bed watching TV a few steps away, I spoke to her.

"How's Olivia?" I asked.

"She's doing better... she told me you talked to her about your dad being gone." I could hear the smile in her voice. "Thank you for that, Dylan."

"You're welcome. I just wanted to help ... she seemed like she was upset. She is a smart kid though. She found my favorite hiding place and you all haven't even been here that long."

"She was upset. But thank you, and she is a little trickster, that's for sure. How's the hunt for your mother going?"

"So far it's been dead ends, but we got a lot done today. I feel good about finding her... I don't know what we'll find when we do find her, though." Glancing over my shoulder for a second to make sure Chris wasn't listening, I continued, "I'm worried what will come of Chris, though, if we don't like what we find."

"Does he seem pretty determined it'll be good?"

"Yeah," I replied with a sigh. "She left for a reason... and never came back for us... I'm scared to know that reason."

"It could be hard for the both of you, but at least you are there for Chris if he finds out some bad stuff."

"Yep. I'm here for Chris..." My words trailed off.

"You want to be there for him, Dylan, you know that. How long are you going to be in Lincoln City?"

"I don't know, Lenny called and told me he put a check in the bank for us. We could be here for a while."

Her voice was soft. "I see…"

"I know it sucks. I want to see you again," I assured her.

"We just saw each other yesterday," she laughed before she got quieter. "But I feel the same way. I want to be near you."

I smiled as the words came off her lips. She might have been hundreds of miles away from me, but I felt so close to her right in that moment.

JUNE 01, 2011

Days turned into weeks and weeks into months as we continued the search for our elusive mother. We even got jobs down at a local surf shop on the pier just to help fill the time while we waited for calls back from the flyers we put up all over the towns that ran along the Oregon coastline. I kept in touch with Ally weekly by phone calls. Every talk was unique and we never ran out of discussion. It was nice getting to know her more through talking, but it pained me deeply not be near her. I sent a few seashells to Sammy and Olivia in the mail, just letting them know that I was thinking about them. I was anxious to get back to my life in Chattaroy, but my brother and I were determined to find the woman who gave birth to us before we would go back to our lives.

Getting back to the hotel one late afternoon after my shift at the surf shop, I stopped by the office to check for any messages that might have come in.

"Hey, Gus," I said.

"Hey, you got one," he replied.

My eyes lit up. "Really?" I rushed up to him at the counter. "What town?"

"It wasn't from your flyers. It was your uncle Lenny. And by the way, your monthly rate is going up."

"Oh," I replied. "I'll give him a call when I get back to my room. Our rate is going up? Why?"

"The owner is increasing it for the summer months. Here's your invoice," he said, handing it to me. "Chin up, buddy," he added. "You'll find your mom."

I smiled as I exited the office. Walking across the parking lot to our hotel room, I kicked off my sandals outside and went in to go shower before Chris got off work. When I shut the shower off, I heard the phone ring in the other room. Rushing from the bathroom with a towel around my waist, I hurried over the phone on the night stand between the beds.

"Hello?" Every time the phone would ring during those months, Chris and I would always be excited at the thought that it could be the phone call that leads us to our mother. We just couldn't give up hope.

"Hey, it's Lenny," the voice on the other end said.

I sighed, sitting down on the edge of my bed. "I was about to call you back… Why are you calling again? I get it

Lenny... you want us back in town-"

"Dylan, stop. It's not that. I found a letter in your Dad's stuff. He got one from your mother a while back."

"What?" I said in shock. "How'd you not find it before?"

"It was inside an old cookie jar down in that room. Why would I look in a cookie jar for a clue about your mom?"

"Okay, okay, I get it. What's it say?"

"It says here she is going by the name Aubrey and is staying on 6523 Sycamore Ave. At least that's the return address on the envelope."

"Sweet!" I shouted. I grabbed the pen and notepad we kept by the phone and jotted down the address and name. "That's strange Dad didn't give us her real name or fake name... or whatever."

"Just a moment, Dylan." He pulled his face away from the phone and began talking to someone in the background.

As he was away, I couldn't help but sigh heavily with relief and smile. We had finally found her! We have an address! Glancing over at the alarm clock on the nightstand, I saw it was 5:04pm. Chris should be getting back from the surf shop soon and we could head right over to Mom's and get this figured out once and for all.

"I'm back," Lenny said. "I gotta run, but hopefully that sets you in the right direction."

"Thank you so much Lenny!"

"No problem. I had to take a double take at it myself and give my arm a little pinch to make sure I wasn't dreaming. I've been searching high and low through everything of your Father's and I just stumbled across it by accident."

I laughed. "Good accident to have!"

"I know! I'm happy for you boys to finally meet her! Take care, Dylan."

"You do the same!" I replied excitedly and hung up.

I jumped up and ran into the bathroom to get ready. I felt an extra little kick in my step as I began shaving. Realizing about half way through my shave I should call Ally, I rushed out of the bedroom and over to the phone.

"Hello?" Jess answered.

"Ally there?"

"She's not..."

"Okay."

"What's up, Dylan? What's going on? You sound excited."

"Nothing," I replied. "I'll talk to you later, Jess."

Hanging up, I went and finished shaving and getting ready. I didn't want to tell Jess we'd be coming back, I wanted the first person I told back home to be Ally. I couldn't stop smiling as everything with Chris and my mom was finally falling into place for us.

Hearing the hotel door open, I cracked the bathroom

door and said, "I have some good news buddy."

"What is it?" Chris asked, walking over to the mini fridge next to the entertainment stand.

"We have an address for Mom!"

"No way!" He replied. He ran over to the bathroom door. "It's really her?"

"Yeah, I think so."

"How?"

"Lenny found a letter from her to Dad."

"Oh man, I am so relieved," Chris replied with a sigh followed by a laugh. "I was starting to feel like it was a dead end journey. This has been an adventure but I need some fruits of our labor man."

"Yeah, I felt that in March," I replied.

"I'm glad you stayed, Brother," he replied just on the other side of the bathroom door.

Smiling into the mirror as I shaved, I said, "So am I."

Arriving to the house, Chris and I couldn't help shaking a little from the nervousness we both felt. We had spent months looking for this woman, our mother, and meeting her had finally arrived. I think a small part of us both knew we built it up to be this big thing and no matter what happened, it was going to be a letdown.

"You knock," Chris said, turning to me at the door.

"What? Why? You knock. You were the one who ran away from Chattaroy to come here."

"Whatever; you followed me here, dude."

Suddenly the door opened. It was a woman with sandy blonde hair. Recalling the pictures, I knew right then it was her. Chris and I both stood idly without saying a word.

"Yes? Can I help you?" She asked. "If you are missionaries, we already attend Calvary Baptist. And honestly anything you're selling we don't need, I hope you both have a wonderful day though…" She began shutting the door.

"No, we aren't missionaries or selling anything," I replied quickly before she could get the door shut.

Looking behind us at the car, she looked again at us. "Then who are you?"

"Are you Aubrey? Previously known as Elyse Miles?" Chris asked.

Her eyes widened. She glanced over her shoulder inside for a moment and then pushed the screen door open and stepped out, shutting the front door behind her. "Who are you? Tell me now."

"I think we're your sons," Chris said with a shaken voice.

I searched her face for some sort of response in her body language as she compiled her thoughts. She was speechless for moment as she covered her mouth with both her hands, and then she said, "What?"

"I said I think we're your-"

Interrupting Chris, she said, "No, I mean what do you want?"

"What do we want?" I asked defensively.

Calmly, Chris said, "We wanted to meet you, and to know why you left us."

"Mom," a girl said looking outside from the window.

"Yes, Jenny, what is it?" she said, smiling over at her.

"Can Megan and I make some chicken nuggets? We're getting hungry and Dad said you weren't cooking anything for dinner."

"Yes, just make sure you make some for your brother," she replied.

"He's twenty eight; he can make his own food," the girl argued.

"Just do it," she retorted.

Sighing, the teenage girl rolled her eyes and left the window.

Aubrey looked back at us. "I didn't leave, I returned."

"What's that mean?" Chris asked.

"Mom… where's the cookie sheet?" the teenage daughter came back over and asked at the window.

"Should be in the dishwasher," she replied. Turning back to us, she asked, "Could we meet for a cup of coffee later tonight? I can explain things better to you then. Let's do the Home Again Diner over off Main Street, about eight?"

"Sure," I replied.

"Just tell us why you left," Chris insisted.

"I didn't leave, I returned, and I honestly can't do this right now. I will talk to you then."

Chris left the steps infuriated and kicked a lawn gnome as he cut through the grass back over to his car. "Thanks," I replied. Chasing after Chris, I stopped him from getting into the driver seat.

"Stop it, Dylan, get out of my way," he said steaming.

"No, you can't drive like this; let me."

Dropping the keys, Chris went around the front of the car and got in. As he glanced over at the house, I saw him glare, angered.

"Chill out, man," I said.

"I can't. She was rude as all get out. And I even kept my cool, for a minute. But did you see that? She has a daughter, and an old son it sounded like! She has this whole other family, one that she obviously cares about. Why doesn't she care about us?"

"I don't know, Chris; those kids could be from a new

marriage. We'll get some answers tonight."

Going over to the diner early, we ate a meal as we waited for eight o'clock to come around. After we finished eating, we began talking about our mom again.

"She didn't seem very nice," Chris said.

"Yeah, that whole 'what' thing kind of worried me. I don't know how good this conversation is going to go, Bro," I replied.

He nodded. "You said before that she probably left for a reason, I hope it's a good one though, she's our mom..."

Interrupting our conversation, Aubrey slid into our booth. "It's not good to talk about your mother that way," she said smiling. With our lack of smiles on our face, we must have made her a little uncomfortable. She continued, "Jeez... lighten up, life isn't that bad."

"What's the deal, Mom? What's your real name?" Chris asked.

"It's Aubrey. I changed it when I moved back."

"Okay. Thank you. And why did you leave us?" I asked.

"That's complicated," she said.

Chris shook his head as he began to get up from the booth, but she leaned across the table and stopped him from leaving. "Please, don't be upset with me."

Sitting back down, he asked, "How? You left Dad and us when we were just in diapers... How could you do that?"

"Markus was getting bad, and he needed my help."

"Who's that? Your boyfriend?" Chris snapped.

"No, my son, here in Lincoln City."

"How many children do you have?" I asked.

"Let me explain it to you this way. I was married before your father to a man name Kyle, here in Lincoln City. I left him for your father because I thought I wanted a different life. I even changed my name to help give me that real feel of a fresh start. Then years went by and I kept thinking of Kyle and then I got a secret post office box in Spokane that Frank didn't know about and started writing Kyle. Our old romance grew back. And when I found out Markus was struggling in Kindergarten, I had to leave to go be with him. I changed my name back. He's my firstborn with Kyle and has special needs. It was all I needed to escape the life I thought I wanted for the one I was supposed to have."

"You thought just leaving and never reaching out to us was the answer? We were your kids. too…" Chris said, smacking his fist on the table.

"I left the life with your father long ago. That part of my life is gone now; it wasn't even supposed to happen. And I have a new one."

"But why? Why did Markus matter more?" Chris asked as tears welled in his eyes. "Why didn't we matter, Mom?"

She shifted in her seat as she shook her head. "I knew you'd be okay with your father; that's why I left. You're bright boys. Kyle and Marcus needed me. You guys didn't. Sure, your father was a little rough, but he was a good dad.

And look, you two turned out to be great…"

"You don't even know me or Dylan. You don't know our life. You didn't care to. How could you know Dad would be the best for us? He was rough; that's an understatement. Kids need both parents."

Chris got up and left out the front door of the diner in a fury. Watching through the large windows as he stormed off out of sight, I shook my head.

"Well, I'm glad you took it well, Dylan," she said.

"I didn't take it well." I paused as I narrowed my eyes on her. She had a smile on her face that cut me deeply. How could she smile at a time like this? I wanted to hurt her in that moment and I used my dad to do it. "Frank's dead."

Her smiled dropped away from her face. "When?"

"Back in February. He never told us you left while he was alive."

"I figured he wouldn't," she replied.

"He said you were dead… And now, I wouldn't mind going back to thinking that." I stood up and dropped cash down for the meals as I went for the door. I didn't want to see the twisted woman again.

Finding Chris out in the parking lot, he had a bottle of whiskey in his hand and he already had a quarter of it gone. "Chris, you can't go backwards because our mom's mentally screwed up. And how did you even have a bottle?"

"Backwards, Dylan?" He snapped at me as he stood

up. "And the bottle… well I bought it a while back when I knew we'd find her. I stashed it in the trunk, waiting for something like this to happen."

"I thought you were optimistic."

"I was, Dylan, but I needed a backup plan if I was wrong. This whole trip was a waste of time." Chris started sobbing as he took another swig.

Grabbing the bottle from his hand, I held it back behind me. He shook his head, "Give it back to me, now!"

"No, Chris. Stop."

He pushed me roughly, causing me to fall back, slightly losing my footing. "You don't want to do this, Dylan. Give me the bottle back!"

"No," I replied confidently. My heart was racing as I feared for what my brother might do next. I was relieved when he didn't swing, but I hurt as I watched him collapse onto the cement in tears.

Bending down next to him, I placed a hand on his shoulder as tears swelled in my eyes. My heart broke for him in that moment. "It's going to be okay, Brother," I said as I let his head fall into my shoulder.

Seeing our mother walking up to us, I shook my head at her. I tried to plead with my eyes for her to just leave us alone, but she ignored me. And then she said, "Chris."

Looking up at her, with his swollen and red eyes, he waited for her response. Again, I pleaded with my eyes for her to leave. My heart began pounding.

She looked at the bottle of whiskey in my hand and

snarled before saying, "Alcohol and fighting? Seriously? You two are the spitting image of your father. I don't ever want to see either of you again."

She turned and paused for a moment before she got into her car. As I watched her, my eyes began to water as her words seeped through the layers of my heart. It stung knowing how little she cared about Chris and me. As she drove off, I turned back to Chris.

Chris dropped his head back into my shoulder and began sobbing as he clenched onto my shirt. Before that moment, I hadn't ever seen my brother hurt so badly and it was the worst day of my life. It beat out losing my dad by a long shot. And as I held my brother close to my chest, I questioned what good God would work this out to be. Scripture has told me for so long that God works everything together for good; but boy, did God have His work cut out for this one. How could a loving and caring God take our father and reveal to us our unloving mother? My flesh was weak in that moment, but God strengthened me in my weakness. I heard faint scriptures press onto my mind as I held my broken brother in my arms. One in particular was from Isaiah forty one, verse thirteen, 'For I am the LORD, your God, who takes hold of your right hand and says to you, Do not fear; I will help you.' Leaning my head against my brother's, I continued to hold him until he was done crying.

JUNE 02, 2011

The following day after the heart-wrenching encounter with our mother, Chris and I left Lincoln City in the rearview mirror on our way back to Chattaroy. I had suspected encountering our mother wouldn't be a pleasant experience, but I never took into consideration how painful it might really be. Our mother was better off dead than alive in my mind now and it was as if she died all over again. What kind of person does that? What kind of mother? Thoughts raced as I got onto interstate eighty four that ran alongside the Columbia River. Glancing over at Chris, he was passed out in the passenger seat with his feet kicked up on the dash and his baseball cap over his eyes.

Chris was a wreck. He hadn't slept the night before, but by the time we pulled out of town, he was fast asleep. He was hurting like crazy and there was absolutely nothing I could do to help him with the pain. I've always felt protective of my little brother and yesterday there was nothing I could do to protect him from the turmoil that our mother wrought against him. It was eating me up inside and every mile marker along the interstate we passed I knew we were going to be home soon. I wasn't sure what that meant for Chris. He had no job waiting for him back home, and he was depressed over our father's death and meeting our mother. How could he not turn back to the bottle? It was how he coped for so many years. I prayed for God to intervene.

Chris woke up as we passed through the Tri-Cities and were now northbound for Spokane. Rubbing the sleep from his eyes, he stretched as he sat up in his seat and collected himself. Glancing over at me, he smiled and said, "It's nice being back in our part of the country."

I laughed. "The dryer air is nice."

He looked out his windows at the fields, "Just has a homey feeling to it all. I will be okay if I don't smell the ocean for a long time."

"I agree," I replied smiling over at him.

Turning to me, he said, "Dylan…"

"Yeah?"

"Where's Dad?"

"He's in Heaven."

"How do you know that? You just have faith?"

"Pretty much…"

Chris let out a demeaning laugh. I knew where he was going before he even began to speak about it. "She said she goes to a Baptist church, just like you, Dylan."

"It doesn't matter, Chris," I retorted.

"Why not? If that evil woman can go to the same type of church that you go to, then what makes you any different?"

"Really?" I snapped at him. "You really think the church makes you the person?"

"Well, I just know you two serve the same God."

Shaking my head, I replied, "God sent Jesus to die for us on the cross because of our sin as humans. We, as humans, are capable of horrible things… but it's God who can and has overcome the sin in our lives."

"You're confusing me."

"Mom's sins don't dictate who God is. Mom messed up, just like every single human on earth."

"You seem pretty okay though," he replied.

Shrugging, I replied, "I'm still a sinner who needs God. Look at it this way, if you aren't perfect you need Jesus' blood on the cross to save you. Mom sucked, okay? I'm pretty disturbed by the entire situation we had with her. But I have to focus on my future and what God wants me to do moving forward. I can't dwell on the past or it'll eat me alive."

Chris was silent as he turned his gaze back out the window. Then he said, "How could God let this happen?"

"He isn't some controlling dictator; he gives us free will, Chris. It's not a matter of God letting anything happen. The world is full of evil and bitterness and stuff that is just downright wrong, but that's either going to make us bitter against God or rely more heavily on Him. In your case, I hope you might seek after God. He wants you, Chris, He wants to take all your pain and heartache away and help you be able to be happy."

"I can't be happy, Dylan. My dad's dead and I didn't go to his funeral because I was off in la-la land trying to find our loser mother." His eyes welled with tears as he struggled to continue, "I didn't even get to say bye to him. He's just gone!"

Putting my hand over on his shoulder to comfort him, I glanced over at him quickly and then said, "It'll be okay, Brother."

"I just want the pain to stop. My chest feels like it's collapsing in on itself. And then sometimes, for a moment I'll forget about it all and then the next second it all comes flooding back through me and about kills me."

"I know," I replied. "Being a Christian doesn't make you immune to the pain of loss or emotional turmoil."

"What good is it then?"

"A relationship with God is far bigger than even I can understand. He puts the stars in the sky and He knew us before we were born. He's all powerful, all knowing and yet gentle enough to help us with the struggles we encounter in our daily life. He cares about you and loves you Chris, more than anyone ever will, even me."

His eyes shifted back over to me as they widened on the last part of my sentence. "He cares more than you?"

Nodding my head, I said, "I abandoned you when you wanted to flee town, I rejected you when you wanted me to stay at the bar that night you got jumped, I failed you constantly… God, on the other hand, never leaves your side."

Chris looked down at his hands as he brought them together. He looked as if he began to think for a moment and then shook his head. "I've done a lot of bad things… I don't think He wants me."

"It doesn't matter Chris, you know that. I've told you a million times there's nothing you can do to earn it."

"Yeah," he replied softly. "I want to be saved."

I was floored by Chris's request. Pulling off to the shoulder of the freeway immediately, I looked my brother in the eyes. "Okay. Let's do it. Let me grab my Bible." Walking to the back of the car, I couldn't stop smiling. This was it; Chris was finally willing to make Jesus his Lord and Savior over his life. *You really do work everything for good*, I smiled as I looked up to the sky. Opening up the trunk, I grabbed my Bible from the duffle bag and journeyed back to the front seat of the car. Chris was breaking down in tears as I got back in. "What's wrong?"

"I just feel so overwhelmed right now," he said wiping his eyes. "I don't know why I'm crying; I'm a dude! I'm not supposed to cry! And I feel like that's all I've done lately!"

"It's okay. Jesus even wept. Tell me, what's going through your mind right now?"

"Just you and how you've tried so hard over the years to let me in on this truth about God and I've rejected you every time. I always felt a little pull, but I'd push it aside because I didn't want to start following rules and regulations for my life. I wanted to be my own boss and ruler. But I'm ready to follow those rules now."

"Those rules aren't required for salvation, Brother. Those are there to help you have a wonderful life and experience it the way that God designed it to be experienced. He does have commands, but those rules you are referring to don't save your soul. God's love, heart and instruction was poured into the scriptures to help those who love Him have a life worth living. Many of those rules or instructions come naturally, as a byproduct to people when they decide to follow Christ and begin learning what pleases the Lord."

He nodded. "Okay."

Opening up to Romans we began with Romans three verse ten. "As it is written, there is none righteous, no, not one." And then Romans three verse twenty three, "For all have sinned, and come short of the glory of God." After reading those I continued, "See, because of what happened in the Garden of Eden, with Adam and Eve eating the forbidden fruit, we are now born into a sin nature. We cannot forgo not sinning. We need salvation from God."

"Okay."

"You believe this passage to be true? You have faith in that?"

"Yes," he replied as he started weeping. "I have screwed up so many times…"

"It's okay, Chris… We all have sinned. Let's keep going."

We continued through Romans and discussed the penalty of sin, Jesus' death, burial and resurrection and then the calling upon the Lord Jesus to be saved.

"Romans ten thirteen promises, 'For whosoever shall call upon the name of the Lord shall be saved.' And in Romans ten nine and ten, 'That if thou shalt confess with thy mouth the Lord Jesus, and shalt believe in thine heart that God hath raised him from the dead, thou shalt be saved. For with the heart man believes unto righteousness; and with the mouth confession is made unto salvation.' "

"I believe that Jesus is Lord and he is my Savior."

Smiling, I shut my Bible and said, "Welcome to God's family, Brother." Leaning over I hugged him.

Releasing from our hug, he smiled and said, "I already feel better, Dylan, like a weight has been lifted. I'm still sad somewhat, but I feel different… ya know?"

Nodding, I replied, "That's the Holy Spirit. When we become saved, we get that. It'll help you on your journey in life. I have it also, which has been a little thirsty for God's word…"

"What?" Chris asked confused.

"It just means we need to nurture the Holy Spirit that lives within us. We need to read our Bibles, pray and really get into walking for Christ."

"Can we do that together?" Chris asked.

I nodded. "I'd love that, Brother." I smiled.

"That's fantastic," he said with a smile. "I'm so excited!"

Pulling back onto the freeway, we continued on our way back home to Chattaroy. On the rest of the trip, Chris asked me all sorts of questions about the faith and being a Christian. He was full of energy and passion for the Lord, reminding me of my early days of Christianity. I loved seeing this; never in my wildest dreams would I have imagined the trip ending like this. I might have re-lost my mother in my mind, but I gained my brother in eternity. It was worth it.

Arriving back home at about six o'clock that evening, we unloaded our stuff and decided to hit the Wagon Wheel for dinner. Chris had mentioned on the drive he'd like to see Elly again and maybe rekindle things between the two of them. I wasn't in any mood to go to the grocery store and cook anyways.

"Hey strangers, been awhile..." Elly said, cautiously greeting us as we walked in.

"Hey..." Chris said delicately. "Could we talk?" He asked, digging his hands further into his jean pockets. I knew it was hard for him to muster the courage to talk to her, and it was a big moment for him.

"I'm working Chris, plus I'm with Mitch now, I'm sure he wouldn't want me going off talking to you."

"Okay," he replied softly. There was no anger in his tone; he just seemed to accept what she said. I loved seeing how Jesus was already making a difference in his life, and I think Elly noticed a change to, judging by the surprised look in her eye at his soft response.

Leading us over to a booth, she left us with menus and went back up to the podium at the front of the restaurant. I noticed she turned and looked back at Chris on her way away from the table, but he didn't catch it. "I wouldn't give up on that one," I said, opening my menu.

He glanced her direction. "She's with someone new."

"Yeah, but I still wouldn't give up."

"We'll see," he replied with a smile.

As we were finishing our meals, Missy came out to our table and joined us. She slid in next to Chris.

"So… how'd it go seeing your mom?"

Shaking my head, I said, "Not so great."

"Your father never spoke much of her. I had seen her a few times when they came into the Wagon Wheel back in the day. She seemed like a good mom with you two."

"Well, she sucks now," Chris replied.

Missy turned and looked at him. "Did she say why she left?"

I sighed. "Yes. She had a different family back in

Lincoln City with her first husband. She left this life behind to go be with them."

"Seems a bit cold."

"Yeah..." Chris said.

"You know you hear about these crazy women who kill their kids, abandon them, and so on... but you never really understand how a mom could do anything like that."

"I think it's just one of those things you can't really explain with a reason. We, as humans, love to know why things are the way that they are," I replied. "But really, you just have to trust God to help you through it."

"I agree," Missy replied.

"I got saved," Chris added excitedly.

"Congratulations!" Missy said giving him a hug. "That's great news Chris! I can't believe it! Your father would be so happy to hear that!"

I nodded and smiled. "He'd be proud you came around to the faith he hadn't had until later in life."

"The guy was kind of a jerk for many years, but it makes me happy knowing he'd be proud of at least one decision in my life," Chris said.

"Hey, he'd be proud of you not drinking too," I added.

"You quit the bottle?" Missy asked, with a raised brow.

"Sure did," he replied, glancing over at me. "Well, I had one hiccup after seeing our mother, but I'm done with that now."

"That is amazing, Chris!" Missy said. Glancing towards the kitchen area, Missy's eye was caught by something. Giving Chris another hug she said, "You have my number if you need anything, I know it's hard at first. You boys take care."

As she headed back towards the kitchen, Chris said, "She's a kind woman; kinda wish Dad would've fallen for her."

"Yeah, you and her both, she loved him up until the end."

"She could have called the cops and got me arrested so many times," he added.

"Yep," I replied. "She's been gracious to the both of us."

Nodding, he said, "I feel like I'm more aware of others around me now."

"Good," I said with a grin.

As we headed for the front door, Elly came up to us. "Hey, we're having a big barbeque out at Roy's tomorrow. You two should come."

Chris looked over at me with a smile. I nodded, and said, "We'll be there." Pushing open the door to exit, I let Chris go first and as he went through the door, I glanced behind me towards Elly to say bye when I caught a glimpse of Ally up at a table in the bar area with some guy. That's strange, who's that? I wondered as I continued outside with Chris. "I just saw Ally with some guy in the bar area back there."

"Really?" Chris replied, stopping. "Does she even know you're back yet? Go talk to her, you haven't seen her in a while."

"I can't do that... what if she's on some kind of date or something?" I asked.

"You're crazy about her; you need to fight for your gal."

Shaking my head, "I don't want to ruffle feathers; I'll talk to her another time. I didn't talk to her a whole bunch while we were in Lincoln City." I continued walking to the car.

Shaking his head, Chris caught up with me on the way to the car. "Weekly isn't a whole bunch? Dylan, we never even talked to Dad weekly."

"I know, but, I don't feel like it's right."

"You gotta stand up for what you want."

"Today's not the day to take a stand. We already had a victory today with you getting saved."

"We're on a roll!" Chris responded quickly. "Come on."

Shaking my head as I looked back, I said, "Nah..."

"It's your journey, dude," he replied, getting into the car.

I liked Ally a lot, but seeing her with someone else made me feel like it might not be as mutual as I thought it was. Our sweet conversations on the phone while I was in Lincoln City sometimes ran into the wee hours of the morning, but was I just an easy distraction?

JUNE 03, 2011

Waking before the sun even had a chance to get up the next day, I had the coolness of the night lingering around the house that morning. After I shut every window to help trap the cold air, I turned on the news to catch the weather. It was going to be a hot one today for Chattaroy, hitting upwards of ninety seven degrees, the hottest day on record for the year.

Pouring myself a cup of coffee, I took it with me out to the shop that morning to start working on my next project for the inn, the bed frames. Flipping on the light, I took in a deep breath and let myself absorb that feeling of being where I belonged. Letting my eyes follow around the shop, I looked at my workbench, my lathe, my story sticks and all my other woodworking tools. This was where my heart was and I had missed my shop over the last few months.

Noticing a barrette lying next to a stack of wood, I picked it up and inspected it. Glancing around, I wondered whose it might be. Ally was the only girl who had been here; it had to be hers. Walking over to the phone on the wall, I caught a glance out the door of the still dark sky and decided I better not call her this early. I set it down on the workbench and then proceeded to gather wood for the bed frame I needed to build.

A few hours later, I took a break to call her. Roy answered the phone and started telling me about how Levi needed an extra set of hands out in the field with the hay this year, and I told him Chris would probably be more than willing to help out. He was about to get Levi on the phone when I had to stop him.

"Wait, could I speak with Ally instead?" I asked.

"Oh… well of course," Roy replied.

"Hello?" Ally said into the phone, I could hear her walking outside, shutting the door behind her.

"Hey," I said.

"Dylan! So good to hear from you. It's been a few days now…"

"I tried calling you to let you know we were coming back to town… and about finding my mom, but you weren't available either time."

"Yeah, it's just been crazy busy, but Elly did tell me you were back."

"I saw you last night on my way out of the Wagon Wheel..." I didn't feel comfortable asking who she was with.

"Oh, you did?" She sounded surprised. "Well, that was Adam I was with, if you were wondering..."

"Oh... and yeah, I was kind of wondering. What's he doing here?"

"He's just in town to pick up the kids and take them back to Atlanta, he drove."

"That's a lengthy drive."

She sighed. "I know, I tried telling him flying them would be easier, but he insisted on driving. He said he wanted to enjoy the drive. I think he's losing it." She laughed a little.

"Well that's good they are getting to see their dad."

"Yeah... Is that why you called? You wanted to know who I was with?"

I laughed. "No, I found a barrette in my shop and I figured it was yours. There are not a lot of women who come into my shop."

"Oh, well, I have dozens of barrettes. You can toss that."

"Okay," I replied. "How long is Adam in town for?"

"I don't know exactly... He got here a couple days ago, and I think he's going to be leaving in a day or two. The trip is pretty long; he needed a break between getting here and leaving."

"Understandable."

"I'll see you at the barbeque? Right?"

I hadn't thought of that. Seeing Adam felt like it could be a little uncomfortable, but I hadn't wanted to cancel my appearance over the fact of him being there. "Yeah, I'll be there."

Hanging up the phone, I felt an uncomfortable feeling settle in the pit of my stomach. Why do I feel like I have some kind of claim on Ally? We had only gone on one date and I had been gone for months. Plus, Adam is Sammy and Olivia's father. I had no right to feel the way I did. Distracting myself from my own thoughts, I picked up the phone and called Lenny.

"Hey, could I swing by the inn and take some more measurements? I need the measurements for the backboards on the beds."

He seemed distracted for a moment and then said, "Sure. I want to chat with you anyways."

"About the whole Mom visit? Sorry about not calling you, it was hard."

"Yeah, don't worry about it, Dylan. I'll see you soon."

Hanging up the phone, I headed in the house and found Chris had woken up. "Levi needs another set of hands over at Roy's place with bucking bales, so that should keep you busy at least through the summer," I said to him as I refilled my coffee in the kitchen.

Nodding, he smiled, "Awesome. Does Roy want me to call him?"

"You could probably just chat him up tonight at the barbeque."

"Alright."

"I'm going over to the inn to take some measurements. You want to come see that treasure room of Dad's I kept telling you about in Lincoln City?"

"I'm okay, I'm going to probably start on some laundry and get this house cleaned up. I messed it up pretty bad before I left town. Hey, Dylan?"

"Yeah?"

"Don't forget to grab the mail from Lenny."

Nodding, I replied, "Okay, you sure you don't want to go to the inn?"

Chris shook his head. "Nah... not yet. I will, but not yet."

"Okay," I replied. Grabbing the keys to my truck, I headed out the door. Getting in, I sat there for a moment as I traced my thumbs along the steering wheel. It felt so good to be back in my ride. My brother's car was neat and all, but it wasn't my truck. Turning the key over, I felt the engine roar as it fired up. Putting it into gear, I headed over to the Silverback.

Pulling off the road and into the Silverback, I was surprised to see so many visitors. Cars were lined up and down the sides of the path leading up to the office and the place was packed out like I had never seen it. Trying to find a place to park, I was thankful when I saw someone leaving who was parked near the office. As I got out, I couldn't help but notice people were even camping out in the grass down by the lake, near the boat docks.

"Wow," I said, shaking my head as Lenny came walking out from the office.

"I know, right?" He laughed with a hand extended. He had a pair of sunglasses on, baby blue surfer shorts and a button-up white shirt, and looked rather relaxed. "Come inside, let's talk."

"Okay," I replied, looking over my shoulder at the people down at the lake. "I can't believe how many people you got here."

"I know," He said, opening the door for me to come inside the office.

Walking inside I saw the couch had been replaced with a white wicker one and the walls had been painted a baby blue color, the wood paneling removed. "You seem like you've been busy," I said, inspecting the wall's paint.

"Yep… We've been pretty busy around here. Kept the momentum going. And as you can see outside, it's been paying off."

"Yeah, I'd say." Walking over to the couch, I sat down with Lenny, still trying to soak up the busy surroundings.

"So tell me about your mom."

Shaking my head, I said, "She was cold as ice, man."

Nodding, he said, "Yeah, I never met the gal, but Frank didn't have much to say about her. He was a private guy and all, but if he had something good to say about the woman, he would have said it."

"It's a shame…" I said, shaking my head.

"How's Chris taking it?"

"He took the whole thing pretty hard, but it's been turning out pretty good for him. He finally came around in the God department. He made a commitment to Jesus along Interstate ninety."

"That's good, really good." Lenny replied.

Seeing Ally walk past the office, I looked over at Lenny. "Ally's staying here?"

"She likes me to call her Allison, but no, she's working here." I laughed a little, recalling her saying she has people she doesn't like call her Allison.

"Oh…" I replied. "I had no idea; she didn't mention it on the phone earlier."

Adjusting in his seat, Lenny said, "Business is really good here, but that required some big changes." He looked a bit uncomfortable with his words.

"What do you mean?" I asked, curiously.

"Allison's been leading the redesign of the entire Silverback Inn. All new and modern face lifts in every room."

"What? You aren't sticking with the rustic western feel that my Dad had?"

"Not exactly…" Lenny paused. "Allison said that the modern themed rooms will help attract more visitors."

Standing up from the couch, I felt angry and betrayed as my jaw clenched. "You can't just erase my Father's hard work!"

"But she said-"

"Allison doesn't run this inn, you do and my Father trusted you!"

"Let me show you a room, Dylan, maybe you'll understand better. I mean, look around you. This place is booming!"

"Yeah, it's booming… but he's gone now Lenny and now his inn is to." I headed out the office's front door, with Lenny chasing after me on my way to the truck.

"Stop! Dylan! I know you are upset about your Father being gone, but you can see the changes were good, can't you?" He asked as I got into my truck.

I remained silent as I turned the key over and then said, "My dad was a fool to have trusted you with this inn." Backing out, I glared over at Ally as she was walking over to Lenny's side. Shaking my head, I could feel my stomach twist. How could they both betray me and my father like this?

Driving back to my house, I was livid. How could Ally just go and change everything? She had some nerve to go and change decades of hard work and dedication in the matter of months. And without even talking to me? We spoke weekly and she hid it the entire time. She knew how much that inn mattered to me and she just pushed her way in and did as she pleased. I should have known she was trouble when she charged Levi and Jess for the nursery over at Roy's place.

Getting back to the house, I went inside promptly and grabbed the bottle of scotch I knew was in the back of the freezer. As I took a swig of it, Chris came walking into the kitchen.

"You okay, Dylan?" He asked softly.

"I'm fine," I replied curtly.

"Why are you drinking?" He asked.

Shaking my head, I replied, "I just need to relax for a moment."

"I thought God helped you relax?"

"Sometimes you just need a quicker method to help you..." I felt regret seep through me as the words came off my lips. Holding the bottle back, I looked at it and shook my head. *That's a lie, this isn't right, but I don't care.* Taking another drink, I felt my insides warm from the alcohol as it traveled downward into my stomach.

Chris stepped back from me and headed out the front door. Shaking my head, I said, "I don't have a drinking problem. I'm not in the wrong here."

Then that whisper inside said to me, *it doesn't matter if you have a drinking problem. You know he does and you are becoming a stumbling block for your brother.* More regret flowed through me and I chucked the bottle against the living room wall, shattering it to a million pieces. I fell to my knees and sobbed as I cried out to the Lord to help me.

My father's death was hard, my mother's appearance was difficult, but Ally and my uncle's betrayal was more devastating and unbelievable. I never saw it coming. How could I ever make my father proud with the inn when it's nothing he ever wanted it to be? I couldn't, and I had no say in the matter because it wasn't left to me, it was entrusted to my unfit uncle. Now I have nothing, nothing to remind me of my father, nothing to make him proud.

Collecting myself, I got a tall glass of water and ventured outside to find Chris. I saw his car out by the curb, so I knew he was on the property somewhere. Walking around the corner of the house, I saw my shop door open. Glancing inside, I saw him over in the corner, sitting next to the boxes of our dad's stuff. He was thumbing through old pictures as I approached.

"Remember this one?" Chris asked, holding up a picture of the slip and slide dad had made that ran from the top of the hill near the Silverback's office all the way down into the lake. It appeared Chris was going to let me slide on that slip with the bottle inside and I was thankful for it.

I smiled as I nodded. "I do."

"He wasn't all that bad, was he…?" Chris said, directing his sights back onto the pictures he was going through.

Putting my hand on his shoulder, I shook my head. "I think he was just hard on us because he loved us. That was his own weird and strange way of showing love, no matter how much we didn't like it. Especially after meeting Mom and knowing he kept us from knowing about her... He was just trying to protect us all along."

Nodding, Chris set the pictures down. "I don't want you to rely on drinking, Dylan... I been down that road and it's not one I want to see you go on."

Shaking my head, I said, "I don't want to go down that road either. I'm sorry you had to see me act like that."

"We all slip sometimes. What happened at the inn?" He asked, turning around to me as he stood up.

"Lenny and Ally are changing it all over into this updated and modern inn... They're changing everything Dad built up."

Chris appeared to be upset for a moment as a frown crossed his face. "That's not good..." He said, letting his words trail off.

"No... but it appears to be working for business."

"How so?"

"The place was packed out like I had never seen it before, Chris. There were even people camping along the lake..."

"Wow..." Chris replied. "Maybe it's a good change then."

Sighing, I said, "Yeah... maybe. I just don't like how it all went down, ya know? And to have it all gone. She updated everything, what's left of Dad in the inn he threw his life work into? Nothing..."

"Yeah, but Dad wanted that inn successful more than anything and if it is, that's something he'd be happy about," he replied. "Are you still going to go to the barbeque?"

Shrugging, I said, "I kind of have to, I already said I would. And I don't want Ally thinking it's because her ex-husband is in town."

"He's in town? Was that who you saw her with?" Chris replied with his eyebrows up. I nodded and he began shaking his head as he continued, "That barbeque sounds like the last place on earth you want to be."

"Yeah, but I'm going to go. I want to see Levi and everybody else. It's been a long time."

The barbeque was in full swing when we arrived. I was happy to remain undetected by Ally as I came up the sidewalk to the yard in front of the farmhouse. My heart sped up seeing her though, even if she was preoccupied with Sammy, Olivia and Adam over by the big pine tree just outside the patio.

Levi approached me and shook my hand. "It's been a while, missed ya around here."

Nodding, I said, "It's been far too long. How's being a dad?"

"Pretty good," he replied with a nod.

"Where are the kids and wife?" I asked looking around the yard at the picnic tables.

"Jess is inside with them. The heat was getting them a little fussy."

Nodding, I replied, "I'll have to go see them before I leave."

"They're a cute couple of kids."

"How old are they now?" I asked.

"Just thirteen weeks old, did you forget our phone call we had?" He laughed.

"Nah, I just don't remember the exact day. The boy is Micah and the girl is… Elizabeth, right?"

"Yep."

Seeing Ally begin to walk towards us, I turned away to look for Chris. He was long gone and over talking to Roy at one of the picnic tables. I tried to make a dart for their table, but Ally speedily walked up to me and stopped me with a touch to my arm. Those same waves from the movie theater rushed over me, apparently ignoring my dislike for her in the moment. I just wanted to pull her into a hug, I missed her so much, but my hurt at her betrayal kept me back. Plus the fact Adam was there.

"Dylan," she said, pleading for me to stop with her eyes.

"What?" I said, agitated.

"Look, can we talk?" she asked.

"Why?" I asked, glancing towards Chris and Roy.

"I know you were a little caught off guard about the inn, and I want to talk about it."

"I'm not really in the talking mood right now; I came to visit my friends."

"But, Dylan-"

"Please, just stop it," I said in a loud whisper.

"Fine." She walked away, forfeiting her attempts to talk with me. In my mind she had every opportunity to explain what was going on to me. We talked when I was in Lincoln City and even this morning before I went out to the Silverback. She could have talked then, not now, not after the fact.

Later in the evening after a delicious helping of baby back ribs and fries, little Sammy came over to my picnic table.

"Dylan," he said.

"Yeah?" I asked, leaning down to him to meet him eye level. "What is it?" I asked, glancing over at Ally as she watched, and then back to Sammy.

"Could you show me how you did that coin trick?"

"Sure," I replied. Turning back to my plate, I wiped my hands of the rib sauce that remained and then brought my feet over the bench to position myself towards Sammy. "So the trick, is just that… a trick. Magic's not real, unless you're in love."

"What?"

"Never mind that," I said. "The coin trick works if you have a jacket on. Do you have a jacket you could put on?"

"It's too hot for a coat."

"True, which is why this trick is nearly impossible in the summer." I reached into my jean pocket and grabbed the wooden coin, bringing it out and placing it in his hand. "See, what you do is when you turn your wrist, you let the coin vanish down your sleeve. The way in which I position my jacket sleeve lets the coin travel down the sleeve and it gets caught in between my jacket and clothing, so I can shift my body and catch it a few moments later when you aren't looking. Takes a little practice, but you'll get it. It's just an illusion."

Sammy smiled as he grasped onto the coin. "Thanks," he said darting away from the picnic table.

I smiled as I watched him take off and go play with the other children who were there. He was a cute kid; so was Olivia. Kids didn't care about the drama of life, they just wanted to have fun and spend time with people that were kind and fun to play with. I went and threw my paper plate away when Ally approached me again.

"Thanks for doing that," she said softly. Her voice flowed over me like honey to a bee. These feelings were so conflicting.

"Doing what?" I asked.

"Showing Sammy that trick... I know you are mad at me right now and you didn't let that affect how you treated him. I appreciate that."

"Why would it affect Sammy? He didn't do anything

wrong."

"I know," she said with a sad smile. "I'll see you around, Dylan…" She added as she walked away.

The rest of the evening blew by without an issue. Catching up with everyone and having that hearty helping of ribs and fries, my stomach was full and my heart with it. Regardless of the tension between Ally and myself, I couldn't keep my thoughts and eyes off her the entire night. I was beyond irritated with her and what she had done, but my heart didn't seem to get the memo. Every time our eyes met that evening, I felt jolts of energy surge through me. I couldn't explain why I still felt so strongly for her still, but I couldn't ignore the fact it was there.

JUNE 15, 2011

Finishing up another rocking chair for the feed store to sell, I wiped the sweat from my brow. Another masterpiece crafted, I thought to myself as I stood back and admired my handiwork. Upon finding out about the inn's new direction, I had put in a phone call to Ken down at the store about making more furniture. He said he would be thrilled if I started back up again since all the stock I had filled up the store with had been since depleted.

On my way to go drop off the rocking chair at the store, I noticed Roy's work truck parked outside the hardware store. I bet that's Levi, I thought as I turned into the parking lot to go find out. I had been avoiding Roy's place because of all the Ally drama and I wanted to talk to

Levi about it since I didn't get a chance to do so at the barbeque.

Walking into the hardware store, I searched the aisles until I found the one Levi was in.

"Hey," I said, approaching him.

Turning to me, he smiled, "What's going on?"

"I saw Roy's work truck outside and I thought you might be the one in here."

"Yep, I have to buy a new o-ring for the toilet. It got clogged by one of Ally's kids and I busted the o-ring trying to pull the toilet out."

"That kinda stinks," I replied with a laugh.

"HA-HA, very funny. What's up? I've seen plenty of your brother, but not much of you… Everything okay?"

"Yeah," I replied. "I just don't want to see Ally right now."

"Because of the inn?" he asked. I nodded. "Well, for what it's worth I knew she was helping over there, but I had no idea she was changing so much or I would have told you something."

"I know that," I replied.

"She's really just trying to help the inn thrive. I don't suspect she had ill intentions in what she did."

"Well, it's upsetting. Chris and I grew up there, and for it all to get changed isn't right. There is nothing left of my dad, and it was his inn. That's how I feel about it, anyways."

"Sounds like whatever she's doing is bringing more foot traffic through the doors and that's good. You heard she's moving out, right? She's going to rent out two of the rooms and just live there at the inn."

"Oh yeah? I didn't hear about it."

"Yep. I guess Sammy's been upset about how much the twins have been crying at night… That makes two of us," he replied with a laugh. "I love those kids, but they don't seem to sleep during the night very well. They take turns waking up practically all night long."

"I'm sure it's a bit crowded out there anyways," I replied.

"Yeah, Jess and I sleep across from the babies upstairs; and Sammy and Olivia share a room off the porch of the kitchen with Ally. Somehow they still hear the babies, probably when we wake up in the night and go into the kitchen to feed them."

"Well it sounds like a good change for everyone involved. I thought Sammy and Olivia were out of town with their Dad though?"

"He freaked out and left in the middle of the night… without the kids."

"Oh?" I replied.

"Yeah, the kids were upset, but they are okay now. That was like a week ago."

"I see. Well I better get going; I have a rocking chair to deliver over at the feed store."

"Alrighty man, come by sometime, we miss ya out at Roy's."

"Okay, will do."

Heading back towards the direction of the feed store, I thought about what Levi said. Ally was making a good impact on business for the Silverback, even if it wasn't exactly how my father had wanted it. If I could get over that and focus on the business then it would be easy to forgive her. I don't know why I feel like she took my dad away from me.

After unloading the rocking chair with Ken, he told me my check was in the back of the store on the desk in the manager's office. He had to go work on stocking shelves before the doors opened in thirty minutes and said I could just go grab it. I went through the store and into the back area to the manager's office. Walking inside the door, I saw the check lying on top of a bunch of papers. Picking it up, I was about to turn and leave when I saw an invoice that caught my eye. It was an invoice made out to the Silverback Inn. Checking the items that they purchased, I saw a bunch of orders for my furniture. What on earth? I thought. They were the ones buying my furniture? Finding Ken, I asked if I could have the invoice, he was reluctant at first, but caved and said it was a duplicate he had made for book keeping. He insisted he just knew Silverback bought them, he didn't know for what reason though. I told him thanks and hurried out to the parking lot.

Getting back into my truck, I went to investigate. I drove straight to the Silverback and knocked on Lenny's door. He answered and smiled when he saw it was me.

"Good to see you back here, to what do I owe the pleasure?" he asked.

"What's this?" I asked, holding out the invoice for him to read.

Shaking his head, he said, "Dylan. That's what Allison was trying to tell you, we used all your furniture to help furnish the rooms."

"What? Why? I thought it was all modern and all updated, like you said."

"It is modern, but that didn't keep us from being able to use your furniture. You should really just go take a look at a room. Unit forty two is vacant right now. The key is behind the counter hanging up in the office."

"Is the office door open?"

"Well yeah dummy, I wouldn't say go grab the key if it wasn't."

"Okay," I replied.

Walking through the loose gravel towards the office, my mind was racing. They used my furniture? Maybe this was Ally's attempt to take pity on me and toss me a few bucks thinking I'd be happy? Grabbing the key, I quickly made my way over to the unit and opened the door.

Walking into the room, I felt overwhelmed. Everything was different. The walls were a crème mocha color and the furniture was all black. I recognized the table as one that I made, but it had been painted. The nightstands and entertainment center were new, but matched perfectly with the table. It wasn't rustic and western like my dad always had it, but it looked amazing. Walking through the room, I made my way to the back porch and out onto the deck that overlooked the lake. One of my rocking chairs I made was sitting out there and I took a seat in it. She really didn't do a bad job, I thought to myself as I lowered my head into my palms.

"Hey, Dylan," Ally said from behind me, startling me.

Jumping up from the chair, I turned to her. My heart was racing. "What are you doing here?"

"I'm going to live here. And then the next one over will be Sammy and Olivia's since these two are the only ones that have a joining door between them." Her words were soft and I could tell she was trying to be careful with how she spoke and it made me feel bad that I made her so uncomfortable.

I nodded. "I'm really sorry I got so upset the other day with you…"

"You had every reason to," she replied, looking into my eyes. "I should have told you about the remodeling we were doing… I shouldn't have hid it from you. I was just scared you would be upset, especially without seeing it."

My own desires of making my father proud and seeing his vision live on with the Silverback melted away and all that was left was an unexplainable desire to make Ally happy in that moment. She had no ill intentions and was only trying to do the right thing, I understood that now. "I was upset… but I am over it."

"What changed?" She asked.

Standing up, I grabbed onto her hands and looked into her eyes. "You were only trying to help… and my Dad wanted people to visit more than anything else. These rooms, they are beautifully designed. He would be proud of you and proud of the direction Lenny took the inn. I just wanted it to be me he was proud of and that's what killed me the most I think."

She glanced over at the invoice that was sitting on the rocking chair. "He would be so proud of you; this is all inspired by your work. Did you come here because you saw I bought your stuff?

"Initially yeah…"

"I hope you don't think I only bought them out of some kind of guilt."

"No I don't think that," I replied. Stepping closer to her, I brought my arms around her as I looked into her eyes. Waves of tingles surged through me as our bodies came together closer. The smell of her perfume and the softness of her skin made the world around us fade. I leaned in to kiss her, but she pulled back.

"Wait," she said, disengaging our embrace. She turned and went back into the room. Following her, I watched as she went and sat on the bed as tears started rolling down her cheeks.

"What's wrong?" I asked as I sat down next to her. She scooted farther away on the bed as she shook her head.

Looking me in the eyes, she said, "Nothing is wrong right now… but everything is wrong."

"What's that mean?"

Shaking her head, she said, "You were gone for what felt like a long time, Dylan…"

"Yeah?"

"When Adam got here, the kids were so happy, and I was to."

"Okay? What are you saying?"

"I tried to make things work with Adam again."

"Work how?"

She started fully crying. "I stayed with him in the city one night. But after spending time with him again, I realized I didn't want to be with him. I didn't want to go back to that life."

My head hung low as she spoke. I was disappointed in her, even though I had no claim over Ally, I felt like, in a way, she cheated on me. I appreciated her honesty but this hurt deeply. My heart literally broke at her words, but I didn't want her to know that because looking at her I saw she was hurting even more. Trying to make sense of it I said, "We weren't together, so…"

"I know we weren't, but it felt like we were connecting that night at the movies… and I thought it was going somewhere and..," She paused as she cried more. "I don't want to lose what we had that night and when we looked for Chris… and our talks when you were in Lincoln City. I'm so scared of losing you, Dylan."

Nodding, I said, "So, is it done with you and Adam?"

Nodding, she replied, "Yes… He freaked out and left after I wouldn't go again with him to the city or kiss him or anything. I feel so bad for Olivia and Sammy; I think they hoped we'd get back together. I thought I did too, it would've made it easier…"

"It's only natural, Ally, to want your mom and dad together. I am a grown man and still wished for it while I was going in search of my Mom. And for you to want to make it work with the father of your children... no one can blame you for that. Don't be so hard on yourself."

"You don't seem mad at all..." she said.

"I'm not mad. Sure, I don't like what happened... but I understand." I chose my words carefully.

She smiled and leaned in to kiss me, but I pulled back. "Too soon?

"Yeah, too soon, I'm not ready for us to be something more than friends right now. I need to process this."

She nodded. "I understand, I just wanted to kiss you since the moment I saw you'd returned. It killed me to see you so mad at me for the inn renovations. But I want you to know I'll wait for you, Dylan. I'll wait for us, to see where this can go, because I think this could be something magical."

Nodding, I replied, changing the subject, "When are you guys moving in here?"

"We're waiting for the people in the next one to vacate, so probably in a few days after they leave."

"Need a hand with moving?" I asked. Why was I volunteering? I needed time to sort this out.

She smiled as she dried her eyes and nodded. "I'd love an extra hand."

"I saw Levi at the hardware store earlier; he said you guys were growing weary of the babies up at night."

"Well, that, and Jess was getting cranky at Sammy and Olivia. Every little sound they'd make while the baby was napping was the end of the world. Really, it was just time to move on."

"Yeah, families living together gets pretty tough, I'd imagine."

"It does. How's Chris doing? Jess said something about him not drinking anymore?"

"Yeah, he doesn't drink now and is a born-again Christian."

"Awesome! Has he been baptized yet?" she asked.

"Not yet… He and I really need to get back to church. Well, I back into church and him to church."

"You should come on Sunday. Then you can help me move my stuff over afterwards."

I laughed. "Oh yeah?"

She smiled as she nodded.

"I'll plan on it. Oh, I forgot to tell you I noticed you have Lenny call you Allison…"

She began laughing. "Yes… Ha! You remember that!"

"I do," I smiled.

"He's smart, but kind of a jerk when it comes to working for him. Very demanding and bossy."

"That's uncle Lenny for ya."

"Yeah, Mitch said it's just the type of person he is when it comes to business. Everything else he's pretty relaxed."

"Yep. Mitch? I heard Elly was dating a Mitch, is that the same guy?" I asked.

"Yeah, he lives in Boise, but is here helping Lenny with all the marketing and whatnot."

"I see," I replied. "Wonder why she'd date someone who is here temporarily?"

Ally shrugged. "Maybe she didn't want anything serious, since she just got out of a relationship with Chris. I don't know."

"Yeah," I replied.

I felt relieved that Ally and I managed to patch things up. It was uncomfortable knowing that she spent intimate time with her ex-husband while I was out of town. Was Ally just another woman like my mother and would one day go back? I would hope not, but I had no way of knowing. Part of me wanted Ally more than anything in this world; the other part of me was terrified of her hurting me again. She dealt with the inn situation incorrectly in my mind, and then let herself get close with a man she swore she was done with. My heart yearned for her, but my head made me take a step back and really look at the situation. Was Ally really the one for me? Only God knew the answer to that, and I'd be spending my time trying to find it out.

JUNE 19, 2011

As I got ready for church that morning, I felt an overwhelming conviction of my lack of attendance at God's house. My faith never wavered in my absence of attending church, but I knew within my heart I was forsaking the assembly.

Chris came barreling into the bathroom about twenty minutes before we had to be at church. "Hey, do you know where Dad's cufflinks are?" He asked.

"I don't… Why do you need them? It's going to be blistering hot today, I'm just rolling my sleeves up."

"Oh, you can do that?" He asked with a surprised

expression on his face.

I forgot that Chris hadn't had much experience with church. He just knew that people dressed up and went on Sunday. "The Pastor likes people looking sharp, but it's not required, Bro."

"Oh, I see," He replied.

"Yeah, just skip the cufflinks," I added.

"Okay," he replied, heading back out of the bathroom.

While I shaved, I thought about seeing Ally again. I needed to find the forgiveness in my heart for her in order to move forward. Jesus died on the cross and our sins were all washed away. So many sins, so many wrongs, Jesus made all right on Calvary. This wrong doing, this sin, this situation paled in comparison to the mass amount of sins I had been forgiven of and I knew I needed to forgive her.

Grabbing my Bible off the bookcase in the living room, Chris and I headed out to my truck. As we got in, Chris said, "Dude I feel nervous."

"What are you nervous about?"

"Going up in front of the Church and confessing Jesus to all those people."

"It's okay, man, it's natural to be nervous. Pastor Johnny will do the talking for you."

Nodding, he smiled. "That's a relief. Do you think he'll want to baptize me today?"

"Could be today, or a week or two away; just depends."

"I see," he replied. "I am sad I missed Dad's. I wish he could be here for mine too."

"Me too, Bro, me too," I said, attempting to settle his nerves.

We arrived at the church the same time that Levi and Jess pulled in. As we got out of the truck, I saw Levi with a baby carrier in each of his hands. I smiled as I walked up to him and grabbed one of them. "Let me help you," I said.

"Thanks," he replied. "I'm glad you guys came."

"I'm going to make it a habit again," I replied as we walked up the sidewalk to the church.

Chris added, "Me too! I need this."

"Grats on your decision by the way," Levi said to Chris. "It's been a long time coming. I meant to say something earlier, but you know how bucking bales can be, exhausting!" He laughed.

"Thanks, bud," Chris replied.

Coming inside, we dropped the babies off in the nursery and took our seats in the sanctuary. Roy soon arrived and sat on the other end of the pew next to Jess and Levi. Just as we stood for the first song, Ally came and sat next to me in the pew. I couldn't help but smile inside and out as she joined my side. While I was apprehensive about her, I couldn't help myself from enjoying her presence. I greeted her with a smile as she sat her purse down and picked up a hymnal.

"Sorry, Olivia was having issues finding a pair of

tights," she whispered into my ear.

"It's all good. You made it, that's what counts," I replied.

We continued to worship through praise songs until the pastor took the pulpit and preached.

"Today, our reading comes from Matthew Seventeen, Twenty. 'And Jesus said unto them, Because of your unbelief: for verily I say unto you, If ye have faith as a grain of mustard seed, ye shall say unto this mountain, Remove hence to yonder place; and it shall remove; and nothing shall be impossible unto you.' Let's pray."

After a short prayer, he continued as he stepped down the steps to meet his congregation at eye level. "We live in troubling times. Yes, this is true. And if you talk to any number of Christians out there today, you get the feeling a good percent is looking up at the sky, just waiting for Jesus to come back. That's not a bad thing, but it is not that good of a thing, either. We are called to be Christ-like and Christ-minded individuals. Let me ask you this, did Jesus focus his entire purpose on dying on Calvary's cross? Or did he live his life for others? He was out in the world helping and healing, not locked away in a house saying it's almost over."

Pastor Johnny clicked a button on a remote from his pocket and the lights dimmed as an image of a mustard seed came up on the wall behind him. "A mustard seed is small, and in our world today, the smaller something is, the less power it has. But this passage of scripture illustrates a very different picture. Something small, something insignificant to the world's standards can be something, in fact, huge." He clicked the button again to project an image of a giant mustard tree.

"God can take our mustard-seed faith and, if we are willing, allow us to live extraordinary lives. Look at the scripture again. It says, 'nothing shall be impossible unto you.' What's that mean to today's Christian?" He paused as he walked across the front to the other side. "Personally, I'm looking forward to Heaven and the afterlife, but until I get there, I want to live this life and enjoy the blessings God so desperately wants me to enjoy. He wrote the Bible for our instruction on how to live this life. And while things in this world are evil, it's not news. Give Paul, for instance. He lived in a time where they were executing Christians for their belief. Sound familiar?"

The pastor continued his message on faith until we finished with a Bible verse that summed up his point. "John sixteen, thirty three, 'These things I have spoken unto you, that in me ye might have peace. In the world ye shall have tribulation: but be of good cheer; I have overcome the world.' You see," he said as he closed his Bible back up at the pulpit. "The world might be crazy and unpredictable, but it's through God's promises in His Word we lean on. If you only have faith as a mustard seed, God can help you through anything and everything that might come your way. Let's pray."

Closing the message out, he asked for anyone to come forward who would like to accept Jesus into his heart. I leaned over to Chris and told him to go talk to the pastor about being baptized. He nodded, and exited the pew up to the front. Watching as he walked up there, I smiled. My brother's soul was secured and his eternity with it. I had worried about him for years and always dreamed of the day he would accept Jesus into his heart. Now he was going forward and following in obedience with being baptized, and I couldn't be more proud.

The pastor prayed with him and then talked with him

until he had Chris take a seat on the front pew. Others came to the front and kneeled down to pray at the steps. After the music finished, the pastor went back up the steps to his pulpit.

"Today, we have a young man, Chris Holden, who gave his life to Jesus on a road trip back from Lincoln City." He motioned for Chris to come up. And as Chris walked up, the pastor continued, "His father, Frank Holden, accepted Jesus later in life and just recently passed away earlier this year. I knew him personally and will miss him.

We will be doing baptisms the last weekend in June outside in the back of the church, for anyone who might want to join us. That's the twenty sixth of this month I believe; right Jerry?"

Looking over in the congregation, I saw an older man nod and say, "Yes, Pastor, that's right."

The pastor smiled. "Thank goodness God gives so many people to help his Church! I'd be lost without all the help." He smiled warmly. "Anyway, help me welcome Chris to the family of God by coming by after this last song and shaking his hand up front here."

As the music wrapped up, a line stretched around the entire sanctuary of God's people going up front to congratulate Chris on his decision to accept Jesus into his heart. We all joined the line and made our way up to him.

"I'm proud of you," I said, shaking his hand. He grabbed me for a big hug and I smiled.

"Thanks for always being there for me. I wouldn't have ever come around to Jesus if it wasn't for you pushing it over all the years… and for the example you led."

"It was all God, Chris, not me. But I'm glad you came around. I'm heading over to Roy's to help move some stuff for Ally. Did you need a ride home?"

Roy said from behind, "I'll give you a ride, Chris."

"Okay," Chris replied, smiling.

Patting him on the back, I said, "There ya go."

The sun was warm as we began loading the back of the trailer at Roy's farm in front of the house. Ally might have not brought much with her from Atlanta, but she sure had accumulated a lot since she had been in Chattaroy. Sammy and Olivia were looking bored as they sat over at the picnic table watching Ally and me load boxes onto the trailer. I stopped to take a break and sat down at the picnic table. Taking a drink of my ice water, I looked at Sammy and Olivia.

"You guys want the gift I was going to give you once you got moved in?" I asked.

"Yeah!" Olivia shouted excitedly. Her eyes were wide. "What is it?"

"Yeah!" Sammy said.

"Let me go get it," I replied. The other day when I was

in Spokane, I saw a slip-and-slide just like the one my dad made Chris and me. I immediately thought of Sammy and Olivia. They'd love it and it was long enough to stretch it down to the lake just like we did so many years ago.

Pulling the slip-and-slide box out from the back of my truck, I was surprised when Adam pulled into the driveway. What was he doing here? I thought he went back to Atlanta, weeks ago. He got out of his car and looked at me, "Hey, who are you?" he asked.

"I'm Dylan," I replied. "You're Adam, right?" I asked, approaching him with an extended hand.

He shook my hand firmly, "Oh yeah, you're Ally's friend, right?"

"Yep," I replied. My heart was racing as I worried what he had come back for.

"Yeah, I saw you at that barbeque thing..." He eyeballed the slip-and-slide tucked under my arm. "You aren't trying to get with my wife are you? Because I've been with her for years, man, and I'm Sammy and Olivia's dad. You can't win this," he said.

"Win? I'm not trying to play a game here."

"Why are you buying my children gifts?"

"I thought they'd like it," I replied.

I began walking back towards the house and he followed behind me. Upon approaching, the children came running and screaming. "Daddy!" He smiled over at me and gave me a nod. Ally came out from inside and up to me looking surprised.

"I had no idea he was coming, Dylan," she said. Glancing at the slip-and-slide, she asked, "Is that for the kids?"

"Yeah, Chris and I had one out at the inn… we set it up to go into the lake. It was fun." I handed it to her. "I thought they might enjoy it here while we continued loading the trailer, but it looks like they might be a little pre-occupied."

She looked over at them and smiled. "They do love their Daddy."

Nodding, I said, "We should keep moving and get this wrapped up."

"Are you sure you want to stay? I'd hate for it to be awkward with Adam. He can be kind of a jerk."

"I'm fine to stay and help if that's okay with you. We are almost done here anyways."

"Yeah," she replied. I could tell she felt uncomfortable with the situation. She looked hesitant to go greet Adam.

"Go ahead," I said. "Don't act differently because of me being here, Ally. We're just friends."

Her lips perched as she nodded and headed over to Adam and the kids. They were a family and I didn't want to come between them if that's what Ally wanted. Continuing inside, I grabbed more boxes and continued loading the trailer. As I set more onto the trailer, Adam approached me.

"Need some help?"

I didn't want or need his help, but I didn't want to be

rude, for Ally's sake. "Sure, that'd be nice if you helped. There's a dresser inside that needs moving." I smiled and walked with him inside.

"Sorry about earlier out in the driveway," Adam said. "I'm just protective of my family, you understand."

"Yeah, I get that. I have a brother I'm protective of," I replied.

"Cool, where's he? And where's Levi? Shouldn't they be helping too?" he asked, grabbing a side on the dresser.

Grabbing my side of the dresser, I lifted and replied, "Levi and Jess are at a friend's house and my brother is at home. It's not a big deal they aren't helping, we didn't ask them since there wasn't too much stuff."

"We?" he asked as we moved the dresser out to the trailer.

"Yeah, Ally and I..."

He gave me a sideways look, I could tell he was trying to figure out if there was something going on between Ally and me. "You have any interest in my wife, Dylan?" he asked as we set the dresser up on the trailer.

Glancing over to her in the yard with the kids my heart felt like it skipped a beat. I said, "We're just friends right now. Aren't you two divorced, anyways?" I asked.

"Yeah, she divorced me, but I plan on getting her back. And last time I was here she thought the same."

"Oh," I replied. I couldn't help feeling a bit disappointed in the fact he was trying to get back with Ally. But if what Ally said was true the other day at the inn,

I had nothing to worry about.

"You've got to understand, I've been with her for six years. That's not something that a piece of paper can tell us is over. I want my family back."

"Yeah, whatever Ally wants to do, I support," I replied. "Right now we're just friends anyways, so do what you need to do." I was trying to soften the awkwardness that Adam was bringing to the conversation.

We continued loading the trailer until everything was ready to go. Ally asked me to join her in Roy's work truck that was towing the trailer as the kids piled in with Adam into his car. As we pulled out onto Elk Chattaroy Road, Ally turned to me.

"What were you and Adam talking about?" she asked.

Shaking my head, I said, "Nothing really… he just told me he was trying to get you back."

"Oh…" she replied softly. "I don't want to be with him, Dylan."

"I know, that's what you said the other day."

"Do you believe me, though? You've been acting a little strange since he showed up."

"Yeah, I believe you. But I do worry a little; you just have a big history with him. I have been acting strange because it's uncomfortable having him around. I know that's wrong of me, since Olivia and Sammy are his kids, but I just don't like the guy. I don't know how else you would expect me to act, honestly."

"Yeah, it is awkward and I understand that. But you

need to know I have no interest in him." She paused. "I hope you can believe that."

I nodded. "I do, but don't forget that right now we're just friends Ally. If you do want to pursue him, go for it. I don't want to come between you and your family if that's what you want."

She frowned a little at my words, but said, "Friends or not, I'm waiting for you and you alone, Dylan. I don't care about Adam anymore. If he wants to see his kids, great, if he's honestly here for me, then he needs to not be around."

Nodding at her we continued the drive in silence, both lost in our thoughts.

Arriving at the Silverback, we unloaded the trailer into the two different cabins she'd be staying in and then I was on my way. Adam hadn't left by the time I was heading out, but there wasn't much I could do. I hated leaving Ally there with him, but I had to force myself to trust her. There wasn't any way I could stay and babysit her and him; I had my own life. Seeing her and him talking in my rearview mirror as I left the Silverback, I said a prayer that God would give me the peace of mind I needed.

JUNE 22, 2011

Pouring myself a cup of coffee the next morning, I heard the front door begin to open. Startled, I spilt my coffee a little as I set it on the counter and reached for the closest thing to defend myself with, a broom. Carefully I made my way from the kitchen into the living room with my weapon in hand, ready to defend myself as the door handle jiggled open. To my surprise, it was Chris. He erupted in laughter when he saw me with the broom in hand.

"Were you really going to beat someone with a broom?" he laughed, shutting the door behind him.

I set the broom against the wall and sighed with a relief. "I was ready to," I replied. "Where were you? It's five in the morning, Brother. I figured you were upstairs sleeping."

"I was out with Elly all night," he replied. "And don't worry; we were just up talking about everything."

"Oh, really?" I said over my shoulder as I went back into the kitchen to grab my coffee. He followed behind me, grabbing his own cup out of the cupboard.

"Yeah man, we're getting back together... she is really interested in God after seeing how big of change I had in my life."

Nodding, I replied, grinning, "That's good."

He poured himself a cup of coffee and added some creamer. "I'm really happy about it. I had no idea how much good having God in your life could bring."

"God is good," I replied. "This world is the closest to hell we're ever going to get, and even if it's hard sometimes, God is with us to help along the way."

"Amen to that," Chris replied with a smile. Glancing over at the clock on the kitchen wall, he continued, "I better try to get in an hour or two nap before I go buck bales again."

"You stayed up all night, knowing you have to work?"

He smiled. "It was worth it, man... Today when I'm dead tired, it'll serve as a constant reminder of how amazing last night was."

"Wow, that good?" I replied.

"Yeah, and the best part was there was no sex or

drinking involved. It was just me and her connecting on an intimate level that we never had connected on before." Looking at the clock again, he dumped his coffee out in the sink and began leaving the kitchen. "Good night, Bro or morning, or whatever…" He laughed a little as he walked out of the room.

Smiling as he left the kitchen, I thought of him and Elly getting back together and it warmed my heart. He was finally getting his life on track. It was a little sad it took the death of our father and our mother re-abandoning us to do it, but that showed me how awesome God is and how he can work the hardships in our lives into something beautiful.

Heading outside to my shop, I had Ally on my mind as I began working on a new chair. She lingered in my thoughts constantly, she, Sammy and Olivia. I wanted to spend more time with them, but I knew Adam was still around and it just didn't feel right to interrupt that.

At around eleven o'clock that morning, a knock came on my shop door. Opening it, I grinned, as it was Ally. But she looked worried as she fidgeted with her purse that hung off her shoulder.

"What's wrong?" I asked.

"I have to leave for a while," she replied softly.

"Why?" I asked, concerned.

"I'm going back to Atlanta," she replied.

My heart stopped. I turned around and went back to my workbench, leaving the open door. She came inside.

"It's not what you think, Dylan. I need to go back and get my Mother's stuff out of storage. I knew it had to be done... I've just been putting it off. Adam told me he already removed his stuff out of the unit and mine needs to go now so he can get rid of the monthly bill."

"I see," I replied softly as scenarios whirled around in my mind. "Just seems random, Ally. He just shows up and says you gotta come get that stuff out of storage?"

"I don't have interest in him, Dylan, I promise you," she said placing her hand on my shoulder. "I think he's trying to spend time with me and coax me into being with him. And that won't happen... It's over, I promise."

Waves rushed over me at her touch. It was so comforting and terrifying all at the same time. I felt so drawn to her right then and I turned to her, pulling her in close to me. As I pushed a strand of her hair back behind her ear, I looked deeply into her eyes and then kissed her. Her lips were soft and inviting and as I released, I caught her smiling. "I'm sorry... I don't know what came over me," I said.

She shook her head as she continued smiling and leaned in. "I'm glad you did." Wrapping her arms around me, she dropped her purse as we continued to kiss.

I got that same feeling that I did at the movie theater. She felt like she was mine and I forgot about everything else in the world for just a moment. Then, my thoughts took me back to worry.

"What's wrong?" she asked, somehow seeing the concern in my face.

I deflected, "Nothing, I just have some more work to

get done."

"Okay, well I'm leaving tonight. I'd like to see you before I leave. And I'm sure Sammy and Olivia would, also."

"Alright, and what time are you going?"

"We're going to be traveling through the night to let the kids sleep in the back. So around ten or eleven."

"You're driving?" I asked surprised.

"Yes, Adam still has his car…" She paused. "We can fly out in the morning if that'd be more comfortable for you."

"Why are you catering to how I feel, Ally? We don't have much of a relationship. Why's how I feel matter so much?"

She stepped closer to me and touched my arm softly. Her perfume filled my nose and relaxed me as I waited for her to speak. "Dylan, I like you a lot… We haven't been on a bunch of dates or hung out for slews of time, but I know what I need and want in a man, and you are it. You're a faithful man of God and you inspire me to be a better person. I know all about those secret trips you made to people's houses, leaving food for them on the porch."

She must have found the journals I couldn't find from back when I was just a young teenager. I had found the majority of them before I left the inn, but there were still a few I couldn't locate. "Where'd you find the journals?"

"Tucked away under a loose floor board in the back room of the office. I hope you are not upset that I read them."

"No, that's fine... I was just a kid."

"And even at the age of thirteen you had a heart for the Lord and devoted yourself to helping others. You're so inspiring... every little aspect about you, Dylan. I have faith that we could have an amazing life together someday. I don't want to lose you... I made a mistake with Adam once and almost lost you then... I won't let that happen again."

"Well, if you want to drive, drive. I'm not going to lose interest because you drove with your ex-husband back to Atlanta. Do what you think is best, Ally."

"Okay..." she said quietly as she picked up her purse from the floor of my shop. "I'll see you around."

Walking out from my shop, I waved as I watched her pull out of the driveway. I needed to talk to someone about all this, and I knew just the guy to call--Levi. Walking over to my shop's phone, I called out to Roy's place.

"Dylan," Levi answered.

"Hey buddy, could we meet up? I need some advice."

"Well, I gotta buck bales here in a couple hours, but I could let you steal a little bit of time away until then. How about the Wagon Wheel, twenty minutes?"

"Sure," I replied.

Hanging up the phone, I was relieved he'd meet with me. He was the closest friend I had that was godly and I needed some advice about Ally and me. I hadn't dated or been interested in very many girls, and counsel was needed moving forward.

⁂

When I arrived at the booth where Levi was sitting at the Wagon Wheel, he extended a hand to shake. "How you been?" he asked.

"It's been good, kids keeping you busy?" I asked as I shook his hand and slid into the booth.

He laughed. "They sure have. What's going on, Dylan?"

"It's Ally…"

"Oh, yeah?" he asked.

"I just have this bad feeling about her and her ex-husband… I'm worried she's going to go back to him."

"Well, they do share a lot of history together, and they have children together," Levi replied. He folded his hands as he leaned in across the booth's table. "I know I haven't been the biggest fan of Ally, but you two look cute together and you look like a couple. As for the ex, honestly, man… I didn't see much going on between them at all when he was here the time before. He slept in the living room on the couch and she only talked to him out of a necessity. I think she's into you."

I was relieved to hear that, but it didn't relax me about

the long road trip across the country together. "They're going to drive back to Atlanta together."

Levi shook his head. "I don't think Ally could do that."

"She told me this morning she was, but she'd change it for me if I wanted her to."

"So, let her change it."

I shook my head. "I shouldn't have to request her to change something like that... it should just be natural."

Levi laughed. "You're sounding like a girl man. Just man up and say you're uncomfortable with it. You can't expect people to act and behave the way you want them to if you don't say anything. Look, she wants you to show those feelings she's already having for you. She wants to see you make a definitive statement of your two's relationship. Stating you'd prefer her to fly would communicate to her that you care about her. That's my opinion, at least."

I took a deep breath in and smiled at Levi. "That makes sense..."

"Hey, Dylan, she's a woman of God at the end of the day... Do you like the gal?"

"I do," I replied with a nod. "I'm crazy about her... and that's what terrifies me the most."

"Could this have something to do with your mom?"

"That's out of left field, but yeah... I worry about her going back to him down the line after we build a life together. I know that's crazy to talk about this early in the relationship... but its recent in my mind with my whole mom thing."

"It's not crazy, man. We, as Christians, don't date just for the sake of dating. We're on the hunt for the woman we are spending the rest of our life with." Levi remained silent for a moment as he paused. "Mustard seed," he said, breaking the silence.

"What?"

"The sermon the other day at church, it was about a mustard seed."

"Yeah? That's about faith in God, not in a woman."

"What's the difference?"

"Ally's not God…? I don't know where you are trying to go."

"We just need faith of a mustard seed in God and we can say to that mountain move! You know why? Because nothing is impossible with God on our side."

"God's not going to make Ally any more faithful to our relationship than He did with my mom and dad."

"Having a relationship with God is a nice touch, but you're right, Dylan." Levi leaned in more. "You know what God does though? He will be there with you every step of the way. So you can step forward with your life without fear. Could Ally turn out like your Mom? Yeah, she technically can. She could also not. She could be the woman you have been waiting for all your life."

Nodding, I replied, "I can't let my mom's mistakes in her past ruin my life today or shadow over someone else's actions."

"Exactly," Levi said, leaning back in his seat as Trisha set down our cups of coffee. "Thank you," Levi said up to her.

"Thanks," I said to her.

"Dylan," she said softly.

"Yeah?"

"I heard about Chris changing... I'm really happy for him. And I hope things don't have to be weird between us."

Shaking my head, I replied, "It's not weird, Trish. I'm fine with it."

"I started going to Christ Community in Spokane," she said with a smile. "I used to go to church but fell away from going a few years back. Seeing God change Chris like he has really made me want to go back to the faith. And the way you helped him... You're a really good brother."

"Thanks," I replied.

She walked away and as she did, Levi leaned across the table. "See that?" he asked.

"What?"

"That's God working these terrible things for His good. You were so upset and worried about your brother's drinking problem and the destruction it left behind... but look--his changes are rekindling Trisha's faith."

Nodding, I said, "It's true."

My talk with Levi was just what I needed to get my

head back on straight and fix my perspective. I went back home to continue working. I kept running Levi and my conversation through my mind. I needed to call Ally. Stopping my lathe, I went over to the phone on the wall and called her.

"Fly out tomorrow," I said.

"Okay," Ally said, I could hear the smile in her voice. "What happened to having me make up my own mind?"

"I know what I want and what I want is you. You asked me what I wanted this morning in regards to flying or driving and I pushed it back onto you, hoping you'd make the right decision, but that's not fair."

She was silent for a moment. "Thank you, Dylan."

"You're welcome."

"I'll call you when I land in Atlanta," she said.

"Sounds good."

Hanging up the phone in my shop, I smiled. Ally was a good woman and I knew I could trust God fully with our relationship. Returning to my work, I continued through the late afternoon with a smile on my face and joy in my heart.

JUNE 26, 2011

It was the last Sunday in June and it was time for Chris' baptism at Chattaroy Baptist. After church was dismissed, everyone funneled out the side door of the sanctuary to the lawn where the old circular feeding trough that they used for baptisms was sitting in the grass. The sun was blistering hot that June afternoon, and judging by all the red hot faces around me, I suspected we all kind of wished we were in that tub of cold water with the pastor. One by one, each person got baptized who had accepted Jesus in June. Chris was the last one to get dunked.

After the baptism, I headed with the crowd back through the church to the parking lot with the sopping-wet Chris by my side. He was wearing a pair of blue shorts and a white shirt, and beaming with a smile the whole way out to the truck. "I'm sure proud of you today," I said, as we climbed in the warm truck.

Rolling his window down quickly, Chris put his arm out the window letting it rest on the door. "Thanks," he said. "My life is so much better now, Dylan… I can't believe I waited so long. I bet Dad felt the same."

"I'm sure he did. That's what happens when you rely on Jesus instead of the world; life gets a whole lot better."

"I always thought this was all just kind of a crutch people were using, but Jesus really does change lives. I'm living proof of that!" He grinned excitedly. "I just want to run through the streets sharing my story with people! I want everyone to know how happy God has made me!"

"Well your story is already touching lives," I replied, looking past him I saw Missy and motioned over to her to have Chris look.

"Wow, Missy came today?" He asked.

"Yeah, so did Trisha," I said. "Your transformation touched lives, Chris, and those people are probably touching others with their own transformations… it's like a domino effect."

"Wow, I had no idea…" he said. Grabbing his towel from around his neck, he set it on the seat between us. "I'm glad."

"Me too," I replied with a smile.

As we drove back home, my heart skipped a beat when I saw Ally sitting on our front porch steps.

"What's she doing here?" Chris asked. "I thought she was in Atlanta for another week."

"Same here," I replied as I put the truck into park in the driveway. Getting out of the truck, I proceeded through the gate with Chris, and he went up the steps and inside.

"Hey you," Ally said, smiling as she shielded her eyes from the sun.

"What's going on? Why aren't you in Atlanta?" I asked.

"I wanted to see you." Ally stood up from the steps and stepped closer to me. She continued, "I missed you."

I smiled as I got a whiff of her perfume. I had missed that familiar smell in her absence. I lifted her hand to my lips and kissed her hand delicately. "I've missed you also."

Ally was turning from a girl I liked into a woman I felt deeply for. That kiss we shared had been on my mind ever since she left town and I found myself thinking of her more with every passing moment.

"Where's Sammy and Olivia?" I asked.

"Back in Atlanta. They're staying with Adam for the rest of the summer. Once he tried to make a move on me and I rejected him, he finally realized it was over and elected to have the kids for the rest of the summer. He's going to drop them off at the end of August with all my Mother's stuff I pulled out of storage."

"He tried to make a move?" I said, cringing.

"Yeah, I shut it down though… He's a jerk for trying that. But anyways, I got something for you." She went out to her car, pulled out a little wrapped box and handed it to me back near the steps of the porch. "It's not much."

Undoing the wrapping, I opened up the box and pulled out the gift; it was a watch. The watch band was silver in color and the face of the watch was a dark blue with silver-colored hour and minute hands that matched the band. Looking up at her, I said, "I love it."

"Look at the back. It's inscribed."

Flipping over the watch it read: Until the end of time, I'm forever yours.

My eyes welled up with tears as I put the watch on my wrist. And she laughed a little. "What?" I asked.

"Is it dusty again?" She replied smiling.

"Dang dust," I replied returning the smile.

Opening my arms up, she came up to me wrapped her arms around me. "I want this forever, Dylan. I've never felt this way about anyone before… I can't stop thinking about you or wanting to be near you."

"I feel the same way," I replied, pulling back from our embrace. Lifting her chin slightly, I looked into her beautiful eyes and leaned in, kissing her. Waves of warmth and love rushed over every part of my body as my lips pressed against hers. Pausing I said, "I love you, Ally."

"I love you too," she replied and then we kissed again.

NOVEMBER 14, 2011

The Silverback's sixtieth anniversary celebration was tonight at the inn's newly-built activity center. Food, music, dancing, friends and family were all in order for the big event. After a seventh consecutive month of record-breaking visitors at the inn, we all felt it was only right to throw a big celebration.

Getting to the inn a few hours before the big event, I headed over to Ally's cabins. I had a jet black suit on and a corsage in hand to go with her dress. I hadn't seen the dress yet, but she at least told me it was yellow, my favorite color on her.

When she opened the door, my jaw felt like it dropped

at how gorgeous she looked. The dress was form fitting and wrapped around her figure nicely. It was yellow with a thick white stripe that wrapped around the yellow delicately; it was perfect. The dress went well with the white rose corsage I got for her. "You look absolutely breathtaking, my love," I said as I placed the corsage onto her wrist.

"Thank you," she replied, blushing.

"Hey, Dylan," Olivia said from the chair in front of the television set. I noticed she had her dress on already, so I went inside and up to her. "Wow, you look just as stunning as your mother, dear," I said.

Olivia smiled up at me. "Well, duh, we are princesses."

"I'm a prince," Sammy added coming out of the bathroom. He had a slick little outfit on himself. Dressed in a nice dark grey suit and a white dress shirt, with a tie, he looked dashing.

"Looking sharp, Sams," I said. "You're going to have to keep a bat on you to keep those girls at bay tonight." He looked confused at my statement.

"Dylan!" Ally said, smacking my arm with a laugh.

I laughed, "I'm just playing. You guys ready for the party?"

"Yeah! Mom said they have a fountain of pure chocolate there!" Sammy said jumping up and down.

"Yep. And Levi's going to be playing his guitar!" I said enthusiastically. "He's really good; he even went out to Nashville a while back."

"I haven't heard him play before," Ally said. "Other than the warm up he was doing earlier today at the inn. I was pretty impressed, myself."

"Yeah, he's talented," I replied.

"Is he purely a country singer?"

"Yeah, I'm surprised you didn't hear him when you lived out there with them at Roy's farm."

"He played in the lower lofting shed when he did play… which wasn't super often, I never went out and listened, though. With Jess being pregnant and then the kids coming, he probably didn't have much time."

"Yeah I'd imagine Jess wouldn't be too thrilled if he was just off playing his guitar all the time," I replied.

She nodded. "Should we head over and see what they need help with? I think everything is mostly done, but final touches might be needed."

"Let's go!" Sammy said darting for the door.

Glancing at my watch, I nodded. "We can head over there now. I'm sure they'd love the extra hands."

Opening the front door, Sammy and Olivia went sprinting through the gravel towards the activity center, dodging patches of ice on their way. Ally and I, on the other hand, took a little slower pace. Looking over at my love in the moonlight, I smiled.

"What?" she asked. "What are you thinking about?"

"Just you and how beautiful you are tonight."

"I love you, Dylan," she said, smiling warmly.

Grabbing onto her hand, we shared the moonlit walk over to the activity center. I thought I loved her months ago, but with every passing day, our love for each other deepened. I was blessed beyond measure with a wonderful woman, and I thanked God every day that I had the faith to trust everything would work out for us.

On the walk over, I spotted a couple coming out of their RV. I couldn't believe how packed out the Silverback was. The entire inn was booked out for the last two months for this event; that even included spots along the path from the road full of RV's and campers in tents down by the lake. Mitch, the marketing guru that Lenny hired, made sure everyone had known about it throughout the entire Eastern side of the state. It was marketed as An Unforgettable Night under the Stars. Levi also made sure to let all the local venues he used to do gigs with know about the party going on, so the activity center was going to be hopping with people tonight.

All my doubts in Lenny's capabilities were washed away over the months as I watched him grow my father's inn to heights my dad only could dream of achieving. I came to grips with all the changes with time and the realization that my father's one true wish for his inn was for people to come and stay.

We walked into the activity center and directly into the banquet hall. I was in awe at how elegant the event was. An oversized gold-colored chandelier hung high in the middle of the ceiling. Each table was covered in a white table cloth, and the centerpiece of each of the tables was a glass bowl filled with water and gold flakes. Floating on the top of the water was a candle. Turning my eyes upward to the ceiling, I could already see the stars through the skylights that sat on both sides of the chandelier. It was breathtaking at how clear the sky was. We got lucky on the clear forecast.

"Wow, this place really turned out amazing," I said.

Nodding, Ally grabbed my hands and turned me to her. "You like it?" she asked.

"I love it. And I know my dad would have loved it, also."

She sighed with a relief as she smiled and said, "Good. I was worried."

"You shouldn't worry, love," I said, kissing her cheek.

Chris appeared suddenly over on the stage from the curtain and waved over at us to come over.

Walking over to the stage, I said, "This place looks great, Brother."

He smiled at me and then over at Ally. "It was all your gal's idea. I'm just the manager who bosses people around," he said, followed by a laugh.

"You liking your promotion?" I asked.

"Loving it." Lenny decided to make Chris the manager a week ago. Ever since Chris started in September, Lenny trained him on all the manager duties, so we all kind of saw the promotion coming his way.

I nodded. "It suits you. I think you'll do an amazing job." I looked again across the banquet hall.

"Glad you like it, Brother," he said. "I got to keep

moving, though. If you want to help, we need to open up the shared wall with the gymnasium and start setting up tables and chairs over there." I nodded to him and then he hurried along and vanished as he went back beyond the curtain. Peeking his head back out, he said, "You look amazing by the way."

"Thanks," I replied.

"Not you dummy; Ally," he laughed.

"Thank you, Chris," she said with a smile. He nodded and went back behind the curtain.

"Did he just hit on you?" I asked, laughing a little as I turned and walked with Ally into the gym.

She laughed. "Ew! Ha. He's like a brother to me since he started working here."

I laughed and smiled. "I know, I was only joking."

Coming into the gym, we found Olivia and Sammy running around in circles, chasing each other.

"I'm going to catch up to you first!" Olivia shouted.

"No, I'm going to catch you!" Sammy yelled.

"Kids are so easily amused," I said as we came over to the shared wall between the banquet hall and the gym.

"Yeah, they really are," she replied glancing over at them. We both bent at the knees and unlatched the wall from the floor. "I'm glad they are happy here."

Sammy ran over to me as we were opening up the wall. "Dylan, you're doing it wrong."

"Your mom's doing it wrong," I replied.

He looked over at her, "No she isn't."

I laughed.

"You are supposed to be pulling up and out," Sammy said as he grabbed onto the wall. I stepped out of the way and he got it moving.

"I guess I don't do this much," I said.

"We had to do it for a basketball thing."

"I see, well thank you."

"You're welcome," he replied. After he finished opening the wall, he went back to his sister, who was going into the closet to grab a ball to play with.

As Ally and I walked over to the closets in the banquet hall to get tables, she asked, "Do you know what Lenny needs to announce tonight?"

"No clue, he didn't tell you?" I asked surprised.

"Nope. He likes to wait to announce things in a big way. Remember? We had that barbeque down by the lake for that announcement about the activity center a few months ago."

"Oh yeah, that's right."

"There have been talks about putting in a new boat launch down by the dock this coming spring, you know, once it warms up and all. We've had some complaints about how the cement ramp is crumbling and falling apart."

"Yeah, that thing has been falling apart for as long as I can remember. I remember someone's trailer tipping over years ago because they hit that corner that's sticking out on the left side."

Ally shook her head, "That's terrible. We need that fixed for sure."

Retrieving the folding tables and chairs from the closet, we hauled them over to the gym and set everything up. While we were finishing up with the tablecloths and centerpieces, Levi showed up.

Coming up behind me, he put his hand on my shoulder. "You like it?" he asked, looking around the room.

"I do, it's amazing."

"You think Frank would have liked it?"

"I know he would have loved it. You going to keep the guests entertained tonight?"

"I'll try," Levi replied with a grin. "I haven't played much since the kiddos were born… but I've been trying to practice since I found out about this gig."

Nodding, I replied, "I'm sure you'll do great."

Levi looked over at the stage. "I better go get set up. I'll see you around."

After dinner, while I was sitting at Ally and my table, I watched her at a table nearby as she was speaking with one of the guests who was staying at the inn. She was smiling that unforgettable smile that I had fallen in love with. I had grown to adore her in every facet of our lives. She was undeniably the most wonderful person I had ever met.

Levi's song ended and then he began playing a slow country song. And so, I went over and retrieved Ally from her conversation. I offered her my hand and said, "May I steal you away for this dance?"

She smiled up at me and placed her hand in mine. "Yes," she replied.

Walking out to the front of the stage, she wrapped her arms around my shoulders. I placed my hands around her waist, and we began to dance. Seeing Sammy ask one of the girls over at the children's table to dance, I smiled and laughed a little.

"What is it?" Ally asked, looking at me.

"Sammy just asked a girl to dance," I replied smiling.

She looked over her shoulder and smiled. "He's such a stud."

"He is," I agreed.

Sammy brought his little friend near us and began dancing with her. He looked at how Ally and I were dancing and mimicked it.

Ally rested her head on my shoulder and said, "I love you so much, Dylan."

"I love you too, Ally," I said with a smile.

As the song came to an end, Lenny got up on the stage and took the microphone. "Good evening, everybody. I want to make an announcement. Could I have Chris and Dylan come up here?"

I looked at Ally and kissed her on the cheek as she went back to our table and I went up on stage. Looking across the packed out rooms, I couldn't spot Chris anywhere.

"Where is Chris?" Lenny asked, covering the microphone.

"I don't know," I replied shrugging.

Speaking back into the microphone, Lenny said, "Chris… Where'd you run off to?"

Everyone looked around for him. Coming into the banquet hall from the door in the back, he raised his hand as he made his way through the crowd.

"There he is!" Lenny said, pointing to him. "Get up here, buddy."

Chris made his way up on stage and stood next to me. Lenny began talking about how long the Silverback Inn had been around and the generations of our family that have had it. Chris leaned into my ear and said, "Mom's here."

"What? Why?" I asked.

Before Chris could answer, Lenny said, "Today I am relinquishing control of all operations over to Dylan and Chris."

The crowd began clapping loudly and I couldn't hear anything that Chris was trying to say into my ear. I felt overwhelming happiness that the inn was being handed over to us, but I worried what our mother was doing here.

Leaning over to Lenny's ear, I asked, "Why?"

He covered the microphone, "It was in your Father's will to give it over to you boys on this date, regardless of your behavior. He must have just had faith you two would figure out life."

Smiling, my heart swelled with love. The whole crowd of people began clapping again. Turning back to them, I spotted my mother in the back, heading for the exit. My heart pounded as I rushed off the stage and wove through the crowd, trying to catch her before it was too late.

Making it outside, I hurried through the snow-covered gravel and up to her. "Aubrey!"

She stopped in her tracks and turned around to me. Her eyes were swollen red and tears were streaming down her face.

"What are you doing here?" I asked, approaching her. "I thought you didn't care about Chris and me, but you being here shows something different."

"The truth is, I never stopped thinking of you two or loving you. I just thought when you came to see me that it would be easier for you two if I said those mean things... But I was wrong for lying."

"Easier?" My jaw clenched in anger. "We thought you were dead, but it turned out, according to what you told us, you weren't dead but you just didn't want us... how's that for easier?"

Shaking her head, she said, "I know it doesn't make much sense, Dylan, but I didn't know how to forgive myself for what I put you boys through when you were younger. You being in my life again would mean I had to be reminded of that every time I saw you."

Lowering my head, I took a deep breath. "You're a Christian, Mother, you should know that God forgives us of what we do wrong."

"You're right, He does. But that doesn't mean we can forgive ourselves as easily."

"Why'd you come here? What is it you wanted to accomplish?" I asked.

"You two are my boys and I want you in my life… I want to spend the rest of my life making right all my wrongs."

"It's going to be hard, Mom."

"I know that, and I'm ready." She came up to me and hugged me as she cried. "I've made a lot of mistakes in my life, Son, but leaving you two behind the way I did was the biggest one of them all."

I felt angry with her and I wanted to hate her so badly in that moment, but instead I was overwhelmed with forgiveness and love for the woman. It was God and his Holy Spirit within me, helping me, coaching me, making me stronger; enabling me for the impossible.

As I hugged her, I glanced over my shoulder back at

the activity center. I knew I needed to get back in there. "I need to get back."

"Okay," she replied wiping her eyes.

"Where are you staying?"

"The Four Seasons in downtown Spokane," she replied.

I nodded. "I'll be in touch."

Heading back inside to the party, Ally was just inside the door waiting for me. "Was that her?" she asked softly placing a hand on my arm.

"Yes," I replied.

"Are you okay?" she asked as we walked back towards the banquet hall.

"I am... I'm a little upset, but I'm okay." Putting my hand around her waist, we went back into the party and joined in on the celebration.

As the party wound down, Chris came over to my table with Elly and sat down. "Hey, could we talk?" he asked.

I nodded and stood up. We headed over to the dessert table and I began pouring myself a cup of punch.

"Are you going to say anything?" Chris asked, watching me pour my cup.

"What is there to say? I assume she said the same thing to you... I'm still trying to process it all. It's hard."

"Dylan," Chris said, putting his hand on my wrist to

stop me.

"What?"

"You have taught me to give people chances time and time again. You showed me by example with Dad… You did it with Ally… You even did it with me. What I'm trying to say is, I can see worry in your eyes about Mom, but I think we need to let her into our lives and our hearts."

Nodding, I said, "You're right, Chris. We need to give her this shot… even if it can end badly… we need to give her a chance. I wanted to hate her so bad when I was talking to her, but God wouldn't let me do it."

Chris smiled and hugged me. "You're a good man of God, Dylan. I only hope one day I can be as great as you."

"Oh, come on Chris, you know me better than anyone. You've seen me lose my temper and mess up. I'm not perfect."

"Yes I have seen you be imperfect, but you always return to God and your faith, Dylan. You've been an inspiration to not only me, but every life you come into contact with."

"Thanks," I replied.

Building a relationship with our mother wasn't going to be an easy feat, but with God on our side, we'd be able to do it. Our childhood was robbed of a mother, but that didn't mean we could hold back forgiveness from her and give her a second chance. God gave us a second chance on Calvary's cross and giving our mother a second chance was the right thing to do.

NOVEMBER 14, 2066

The following years after that night, my mother worked endlessly to build a relationship with my brother and me. And while she was never able to give us what we lost from our childhood, she did give everything she could up until her death over a decade later. We even went back to Lincoln City a few times to visit our half-siblings. And while our mother is gone now, much like the majority of the people I loved and cared about from my youth, I can't help but to smile, thinking back to that night that was so long ago. I was proud of the woman who my mother had become through her own faith and walk with God. His love, mercy and grace were the only reasons why Chris and I were able to repair our relationship with her.

As I sit here on the back balcony of the cabin Ally and

I lived in, I smile as I think about how my mother and she are probably both up in heaven talking with my dad. Interrupting my thoughts, Sammy, who goes by Samuel now, came outside from the cabin.

"Did you remember the party was at six?" he asked. "Everyone is already at the Banquet Hall, just waiting on you."

"Is it that time already?" I asked, looking at my watch. I began to stand up, but my strength failed me and Sammy rushed over to help me get my footing. "Thank you," I said to him, grabbing onto his hand. "Did your wife make it from Portland in time?"

"Yes," he replied, smiling. "She wrapped up her meeting early with the board and had already packed her bag this morning at home."

"Good," I said firmly as I grabbed my cane from next to the rocking chair.

Walking across the parking lot of the Silverback, I marveled at how time had changed the Silverback. The gravel had been since replaced with pavement and the office building was torn down and rebuilt farther away from the lake, which provided more room for additional cabins.

It had changed far more dramatically over the last forty years than ever before, but I embraced every change along the way, as it was for the better of the inn. I still thank God daily that Lenny took over the inn when he did, for if Lenny didn't take over like he did back then, I don't think the Silverback would be anything other than a memory to this day.

Walking into the activity center, I made my way to Chris and Elly's table. Sitting down with a heavy sigh, I smiled over at the both of them.

"Congratulations on a hundred and fifteen years of operation," Chris said.

"Same to you," I replied with a smile.

We enjoyed food, music and guest speakers that evening. It was enjoyable, but I longed for my Ally as the seat next to me was empty. A night like this was especially hard, as she was so instrumental back when the Silverback really began taking off. She was the greatest love of my life and I'll love her until I take my final breath. My memories of her, the kids and our life help get me through occasions like this day.

The air in the banquet hall was becoming rather stuffy, so I excused myself for a fresh breath of air. Making my way out the doors and outside, I looked up at the night sky and marveled at the stars. They never change, just like God, and I took comfort in that fact.

"He does some amazing work, doesn't He?" Chris said, joining my side outside.

"He sure does," I replied, smiling.

We began walking down the path that led out to the main road and I turned to Chris. "I want to be buried out here on the lake."

"Yeah? Next to Ally in the plot along the old walking path we used to hike on, right?"

"Yes."

"I already assumed this, since Ally is there, Dylan," he replied. "What's going on?"

"I just wanted to make sure."

"You planning on exiting soon?" Chris asked with a laugh.

"Not planning, but I won't stop it if it comes," I replied smiling.

As we made it out to the road, we turned back around and started heading back over the bridge. "You want to race? Like the good ol' days?" I asked.

Chris smiled over at me and laughed. "Yeah, sure. I might have you beat now though."

I took off in a sprint--well it wasn't more than a wobble with my cane, and Chris followed suit. His lack of cane allowed him a faster pace and he passed me with ease. As we came to a stop, we both began laughing.

"Guess you finally beat me," I said, panting heavily.

He laughed as he patted my shoulder. "That I did! It only took until you were a cripple to do it!"

I stood up, took a deep breath and smiled. Going back into the celebration party, I said my goodbyes to all my children and retired back to my cabin, for my little race with Chris had exhausted me.

Finding my bed all too inviting, I lay down and took a deep breath. Looking up at the ceiling, I closed my eyes and prayed quietly to myself.

Dear heavenly Father, thank you for the life I have

lived. The people I have met and the family I have raised. It's through faith in you that this amazing life I've lived has been possible. I love you and thank you for everything. Amen.

Letting myself slip into a slumber, I recalled the memories of Ally and me when we handed over the operations of the inn to Sammy and Olivia. It was back twenty years ago when we did it and right after it happened, Ally and I bought an RV. We traveled all over the United States together. Sometimes we got lost, sometimes we didn't, but each road led us somewhere new. And as I fell deeper into my slumber that night, I could feel myself on a new road. Eternity. And I felt an overwhelming sense of peace, relaxation and love overwhelm me in that final moment.

The End

OTHER BOOKS

Love Again

Love Interrupted

The Perfect Cast

Finding Love

Claire's Hope

Subscribe to the Newsletter for special Prices, free gifts and more!

www.tkchapin.com

AUTHOR'S NOTE

When you leave a review on a book you read, you're helping the author keep the lights on. Our books don't sell themselves, it's word of mouth and comments others have made. Simply visit Amazon and/or Goodreads and let others know how the book was for you. It'd help me greatly. Thank you!

ABOUT THE AUTHOR

T.K. CHAPIN writes Christian Romance books designed to inspire and tug on your heart strings. He believes that telling stories of faith, love and family help build the faith of Christians and help non-believers see how God can work in the life of believers. He gives all credit for his writing and storytelling ability to God. The majority of the novels take place in and around Spokane Washington, his hometown. Chapin makes his home in the Pacific Northwest and has the pleasure of raising his daughter with his beautiful wife Crystal. To find out more about T.K. Chapin or his books, visit his website at www.tkchapin.com.

CPSIA information can be obtained
at www.ICGtesting.com
Printed in the USA
LVHW080100080220
646300LV00033B/800